THE ESSENTIAL BOOK OF TEACHER TIPS

Standard®
PUBLISHING

Cincinnati, Ohio

Published by Standard Publishing, Cincinnati, Ohio
www.standardpub.com

NIV® is a registered trademark of Biblica, Inc.

Printed in United States of America

Cover design: Andrew Quach
Interior design: Andrew Quach

ISBN 978-0-7847-3529-9

17 16 15 14 13 12   1 2 3 4 5 6 7 8 9

TABLE OF CONTENTS

TABLE OF CONTENTS

TABLE OF CONTENTS

TABLE OF CONTENTS

INTRODUCTION

"Not many of you should become teachers," warns James the brother of Jesus and a leader in the early church (James 3:1). There is probably not a teacher in any church today who has not had moments when he wished he had paid more attention to that warning! Usually this happens in dry times, when the teacher struggles to find something fresh—not just in content, but in methods. When teaching becomes routine, when it's always the "same old thing," then something needs to change.

Too often the teacher gives up in frustration, and the change is a new teacher. It does not have to be that way! With a few fresh ideas the same teacher can continue in the role of teacher. Learners will appreciate the new approach, and the teacher will once again find fulfillment in her role. That is the purpose of this book.

These teacher tips come from teachers. They come from the front lines, where real teachers struggle to make lessons relevant to real learners. This is not some academic treatise, but a handbook of real-life solutions.

We all tend to teach to our strengths. If everyone in our classes learned the way we do, we'd have no problem. But some of us are visual and some of us are auditory. Some people like to hold and touch things, and some actually like to get up and move around. We all need help from time to time as we try to relate to those who learn in ways different from our own learning styles. This book will help you do just that!

Adults love to talk, so discussion is a good method to use with adults. You'll find tips here on how to lead a good discussion. Adults like to get involved, so you'll find tips here on getting your adult learners involved. Involve them in the lesson, and involve them in ministry—both are important! You'll find dozens of tips to help you better teach adults in just about any setting.

AND THAT'S NOT ALL! If you teach from a Uniform Series curriculum, you'll love the new Teacher Tips website that this book gives you access to (www.standardlesson.com/teachertips). For one full year your subscription is paid, and you can go again and again to find timely tips on teaching each week's lesson. You'll find links to other helpful sites as well as specific activities to use in your group. You'll find opening activities, Bible study activities, and application activities—just about anything you can imagine.

So while not many of us should become teachers, thank God for the few who do and do so responsibly. This book will help you stay fresh in that role. It will help you live up to the responsibility you have accepted.

THE ACTS OF PEOPLE

Making Bible People More "Personal"

by Ronald G. Davis

Although the fifth book of the New Testament is usually called "The Acts of the Apostles," Acts is a book about people: men and women, slave and free, Greek and Barbarian, Jew and Gentile, noble and ignoble. Acts is a book about people who came face-to-face with the gospel of Jesus Christ. The issue in every such encounter was "Will the gospel be allowed to demonstrate its power, or will it be met and resisted by the force of personal will?"

A study of Acts ought to fortify the Christian's confidence in the gospel's power to change lives. The gospel is "the power of God that brings salvation to everyone who believes" (Romans 1:16). The occasions when the gospel is resisted reflects on the will of the person involved, not on the character of the gospel. Students of the book of Acts should walk away from their study confident that the gospel preached, taught, and modeled can work with any person—regardless of social status, religious background, or ethnic heritage.

The teacher of Acts will want to personalize the studies—that is, to make the people of the first century alive and as real as family members and neighbors. Two approaches to making that happen follow. One we will call Label Makers; the other we will call Dramatic Interviews.

Label Makers

Consider some of the significant individuals in the book of Acts: Peter, Stephen, Philip, the Ethiopian eunuch, Saul/Paul, Barnabas, Cornelius, Lydia, the Philippian jailer, and the Ephesian elders. For each one there is a collection of labels that fits him or her to a tee. Developing such a list of labels—some obvious, some not so obvious—is a worthwhile activity for any class. The teacher has two sources for such a list: 1) make the list himself and introduce it to the students for their consideration and explanation, or 2) have the class itself develop the list.

Look at this list of characteristics for the Ethiopian eunuch of Acts 8:26-39: *man, Ethiopian, eunuch, outsider, alien, African, steward, powerful, responsible, literate, treasurer, worshipful, committed, wealthy, humble, hospitable, listener, servant, curious, concerned, responsive, obedient, joyful, confused, open, rider, opportunist, mutilated.*

And consider this list for the Philippian jailer of chapter 16: *callous, obedient, careful, thorough, diligent, wise, responsible, loyal, kind, joyful, hospitable, Roman, scared, homeowner, believer.*

Can you explain all the labels suggested? Can your students? Can you add to the lists? Can your students?

As a teacher, if you have compiled your own list, you could show all the contents at once and ask your class to identify the reason each term would be appropriate; or you could read/write one word at a time, followed by the same call for student response. If you ask the class to devise the list, consider displaying a large cutout of a person on the wall and then asking class members to approach and write their labels on the cutout. (Label the cutout across the head with the name of the person under consideration.) Some will enjoy the graffiti nature of this activity, and having the cutout on the wall for a week or two may help the students remember the study and its applications to their lives.

Another approach to developing such a list is to give each student a three-by-five index card or a half-sheet of paper and ask each to write down three words that could be used to describe the person who is the subject of the study. Cornelius, the centurion, is the subject of Acts 10. Have students read the entire account; then give them this statement to complete by using three one-word responses: "Cornelius was (a/an). . . ." (The optional *a/an* gives the students the opportunity to complete the statement with either an adjective [devout, wise, etc.] or a noun [soldier, leader, officer, etc.]).

After three or four minutes, ask students to read "the one word on your list that you doubt anyone else has" or, "the one word on your list that you think most people included." After a word is read, ask for a show of hands of others who included the same word. This will allow a comparison and contrast of lists and will provide a thorough description/characterization of Cornelius. Labels a teacher might expect to hear most often include *God-fearing, Roman, devout, centurion, generous, prayer*; labels that might appear on a few lists include *expectant, kind, hospitable, baptized, listener, afraid, well-to-do.* For those words that no other class member included, ask the reader to explain his choice. In most such activities, some students will include words the teacher has never considered, and usually they will have interesting and even insightful explanations for the choices.

For some individuals and classes, preparing an acrostic using the key character's name is an enjoyable and profitable "label-making" activity. Such a longer name as Cornelius lends itself to acrostic-making. Consider: **C**ommander, **O**bedient, **R**espected, **N**otable, **E**xpectant, **L**oving, **I**talian, **U**nusual, **S**pirit-filled. Shorter names or titles may lend themselves to sentence acrostics. Consider the Ephesian elders of Acts 20:17-32: **E**phesian **l**eaders **d**early **e**ncouraged (by) **r**eminding **s**ervant.

Dramatic Interviews

A dramatic or dramatized interview presents an up-close-and-personal look at a particular biblical person. A "pretender" (actor/actress) is called on to answer questions about the person being represented—questions with factual responses based on history, geography, culture, and the biblical record, and questions with only speculative responses (though even those responses should have some reasonableness to them). A few props or a bit of costuming can be used, but neither needs to be present for the activity to be effective.

The teacher can play the role of the one interviewed, the interviewer, or neither. Such interviews can be carefully "scripted" or almost spontaneous. Each approach offers some legitimate learning opportunities for the class. The interviews can be conducted in a one-on-one, "TV news-magazine" setting or in a "press conference" arrangement. The latter offers more student involvement; the former may be "safer" and more controlled.

Stephen could serve as the ideal subject of a dramatic interview. If a teacher recruits another person to be Stephen, the actor can be interviewed with such questions as these: (1) Stephen, could you describe the situation that led to your being selected to help with the ministry to the widows? (2) What are some of the "great wonders and signs" you were able to do? (3) Why did the Jews begin to argue with you? (4) How could they accuse you of speaking words of blasphemy against Moses and against God? What had you been saying that led them to make such a charge? (5) When you were on trial before the Sanhedrin, how was your experience there similar to Jesus' experience? (6) Your summary of the Old Testament, moving from Abraham through the prophets, is a marvelously concise history. How did you learn that history so well? (7) Briefly describe your vision of the heavenly throne room. What sort of encouragement was that to you? (8) Stephen, give our class one final word of encouragement. What do you think we most need to hear? (Note that whoever participates in this interview will need to be familiar with the entire account of Stephen as recorded in Acts 6 and 7.)

If the teacher decides to let the class, or a representative group of four to six, do the interviewing, he can prepare and assign questions to each member of the group, he can recruit his panel early and ask them to develop their own questions, or the questions can be worded spontaneously by the members after a brief introduction by the teacher. If the individual playing the role of the Bible person wants to be more confident in responding during the interview, the questions should be pre-arranged, with a copy given to the individual before class. But if that person is willing, spontaneous and unknown questions will probably elicit a more interesting response.

"Getting to Know You"

The words of an older popular song, "Getting to know you; getting to know all about you," state a worthy goal for a study of the book of Acts. Getting to know the people there, learning that they were real people struggling to stay faithful to Christ in an amoral or even immoral culture, and sensing their deep faith and commitment to the gospel—achieving these goals will make the time you spend in class a valuable one for your adult students.

Probably every member of your adult class has experienced a period of doubt and discouragement. (Some may be experiencing such a time right now.) To study the book of Acts is to study those individuals who are now among "such a great cloud of witnesses" and whose example can encourage us to "run with perseverance the race marked out for us, fixing our eyes on Jesus" (Hebrews 12:1, 2). By getting to know them, we can run our race with greater confidence.

APPLYING THE BIBLE TO LIFE
The Second Half of the Lesson

by James Riley Estep, Jr.

Many Sunday school teachers resist the idea of making application, perceiving their role to be a teacher of Bible content and little more. "Students should just make the lesson application themselves," they say. "That's not really the teacher's responsibility." Is that your viewpoint?

Why Teachers Hesitate

There are various reasons why teachers hesitate when it comes to application. Some teachers avoid making application to life out of fear of appearing authoritarian or intrusive into students' personal lives. Other teachers resist making application because they don't want to "step on people's toes." The result in these cases is a Bible lesson that is taught in a vague, general way. In order to avoid controversy, they avoid focus, clarity, and challenge.

If a student is offended by a suggested application to life, could that not mean that the student is living in a way that is contrary to the Scriptures? We recall this warning: "Do not merely listen to the word, and so deceive yourselves. Do what it says" (James 1:22). This means that teaching the Bible text is incomplete without application. Application to life is more likely to happen when the teacher recognizes his or her responsibility in this regard.

The Teacher's Task

The simple diagram below depicts the teaching process in its most complete form. The first step, naturally, is to read the biblical text. From there we move on to explaining its meaning. This step involves coming to grips with what the Bible author intended the original readers to understand (the fancy word for this is *exegesis*).

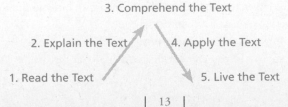

3. Comprehend the Text

2. Explain the Text   4. Apply the Text

1. Read the Text   5. Live the Text

The third step, comprehension, involves helping the student begin to see how his or her understanding of the text can form a general principle of life. This step is your vital bridge between explanation of the text and application to life. When the learner studies a passage and comprehends it (not just memorizes it), then the teacher is ready to move to application of the passage. Until comprehension is achieved, application is virtually impossible because the text is still too "distant" from the life of the learner. Our study of the passage must take us successfully through this point.

We can help our learners form these general principles of life by considering *life parallels*. How does the situation of the biblical author's message parallel our situation today? In those parallels, how does the biblical message address the culture, congregation, and general life situation of the student? It is here the learner should begin to see similarities between the lives of biblical characters and their own regarding circumstances, challenges, and decisions.

Consider, for example, Paul's discussion in Ephesians 2 about the relationship between Jews and Gentiles in the church. That situation in and of itself is probably rather "distant" to your learners. Chances are they have never experienced a conflict between Jew and Gentile in the churches they have attended. Thus the issue by itself doesn't carry the immediacy that it did in the first century.

However, the nature of relations between people of different races or cultural backgrounds is a very real issue in the twenty-first century. In this light, Paul's discussion about the relationship between Jews and Gentiles informs what our response should be to twenty-first century parallels. Now the text is definitely getting closer to our life, society, and world.

After establishing a general arena of application (in this case, race and/or cross-cultural relationships), we ask ourselves, "What specific *life applications* can be made? What are students expected actually to do about it?" As teachers, we prepare for a lesson by thinking through these questions, but ultimately we have to ask how we can help students develop a specific plan for biblical life-change. It is never enough merely to draw parallels for students or have them brainstorm about possible applications before you move on to the next verse. Students must be asked, "So, what are you going to do about it? What changes do you need to make to reflect the biblical text in your life?" After all, this is ultimately how Scripture is to affect students.

Classroom Tips

The next question is "But how do we set this process in motion in the classroom? What's the best way to move from *general life-principle to specific application?*" Your lesson aims for each study should form a good starting point for you in this regard. You should have aims that deal with knowing and comprehending the lesson text (content and concept aims), but you should always also have at least one aim that addresses application (conduct aim).

There is more than one way to achieve those aims, depending on your teaching style. If you like to use a learning-activity approach, you can use that to achieve all three aims. After an attention-getter, you move to Bible study proper; this is where your activities are designed to achieve your content and concept aims. Follow that with an application section that seeks to achieve the conduct aim.

You can also use a discussion approach to achieve your application aim. After helping your learners comprehend the biblical message, you can lead them in a discussion of possible applications of the biblical principle. Students actively participate by suggesting parallels between the situations of the people in the Scriptures with those in our own world today. Your task is to help the students push their comprehension to application.

For example, after studying Paul's praise of the Thessalonian church (1 Thessalonians 1:4-10), you can ask, "How does our congregation measure up to what Paul expected in a church?" After a time of class or small-group discussion, the next question can be, "How can you, individually, help our church become what God expects it to be?" This brings the biblical text into "real life" application for the student.

For an Old Testament example, consider Moses' educational mandate in Deuteronomy 6. After addressing what this text meant for the people "back then," you can ask students to suggest general applications of the biblical text for modern parenting or children's ministry at the church. Classes can brainstorm possible applications, and the more the better! After the brainstorming winds down, you can ask your learners to select one possible application to put into practice in the week ahead. Thus the application can result in biblically informed life-changes.

The advantage of this kind of approach is that your learners will have a greater sense of "ownership" of the action plan because of their participation in helping create it. If you, the teacher, want to retain a bit more control during a discussion (to keep the class from going off on tangents), you can provide the life parallels yourself. You can do this by bringing newspaper or magazine articles that address the issue at hand. If your classroom is equipped to do so, you can show video clips from a movie, documentary, or Internet site.

Keep in mind that after a period of general discussion, the lesson focus must shift to the life of the individual student. At the beginning of a discussion the teacher may ask, "What are *we* going to do about this?" but the question eventually must move to "What are *you* going to do about it?" Asking students to identify a biblical life-change they can make in the week ahead is somewhat easy given the fact that they have spent time discussing possible general applications. Moving from the general application to the specific application simply becomes a matter of determining what God wants each one of them to do about it.

The creation of a specific application also provides a point of assessment for the lesson itself: the following week the teacher simply asks students if they followed through with the application of the previous week's lesson. This builds a sense of spiritual accountability among your class members. When application is done in this way, it becomes a natural extension of biblical study, which is exactly what it should be.

Even if your preferred teaching style is primarily lecture, you can move your class from comprehension to application by selective and occasional use of discussion questions.

Complete Interpretation

As one student has pointed out, "The interpretation of Scripture is not complete until its application is found for the reader in his or her present situation." This means that an explanation of the Bible text must be followed by coming to grips with how that text is to be lived out.

Keep in mind that leading your students to make application of the biblical text in their own lives does not require you, the teacher, to directly make the application *for* them. Rather, your job is to assist your students in making their own applications. That's complete interpretation!

BIBLE ALIVE

Appreciating the Relevance of Scripture

by James Riley Estep, Jr.

Many people today do not see the Bible as relevant. Christians disagree. We affirm the continuing relevancy of the Bible for at least two reasons. First, Scripture is authored ultimately by the eternal God. While the Bible was indeed penned by men, they were not the ultimate authors (2 Timothy 3:16; 2 Peter 1:21). Second, the Bible addresses unchanging human needs and nature. Regardless of advances in science, we still struggle to meet basic needs, to overcome evil, to find redemption, etc. A stroll through the book of Ecclesiastes demonstrates such struggles are not new.

However, most people who ignore the Bible do not do so because of some profound philosophical or historical argument against it. Rather, they don't listen to it because it simply *seems* irrelevant given the way that it is taught. Have we taken a Word that is described as "quick, and powerful" (Hebrews 4:12) and treated it as if we were dissecting a frog in science class? The Bible is not outdated, but our teaching methods may be! Let's examine three ways to make the Bible come alive in our teaching: illustrate, participate, and express.

Illustrate

When you are teaching, make sure to use *illustrations*, both verbal and visual, to demonstrate the reality of Scripture and its relevance for today. People love stories today. The experts at communicating with the young adult generation are fond of saying "The story is the message." While some think that overstates the case, stories that illustrate the message are always helpful.

Visually, you can show pictures or even videos of the geography of the Holy Land. You can use GoogleEarth for this if your classroom has Internet access. Other pictures are useful as well. If you use PowerPoint (or some other presentation software) be sure to include pictures to illustrate your slides. Sometimes a picture by itself on the slide, combined with what you say in class, makes the best illustration for your message. Words on the slide may actually compete with your message, sometimes spoiling the timing of your delivery.

Participate

Having your students participate in the biblical narrative means helping them engage in the activity of that narrative. For example, you can have your learners try making bricks both with and without straw if the lesson is on Exodus 5:6-18 (brick recipes are on the Internet). This will add a tactile element to the narrative, helping your learners sense the text in a way beyond hearing.

"Acting it out" thus requires the learners to place themselves into the narrative. Beyond merely asking, "How would you have felt if you were they?" acting-it-out asks learners to wrestle with choices in a hands-on way. Notice the difference: you're not asking them just to think *about* the biblical text, but to place themselves *inside* it. This helps the learner realize that Bible characters were real people facing real-life situations. There are limits, of course. For example, having your learners make their bricks out in the hot sun is not recommended!

Express

Finally, your learners can encounter the living Word as you help them express it through their lives. For example, you can ask the learner to personalize a psalm, describing their family in light of a passage on community. You also could hold a "mock" elders' meeting in which participants grapple with how to ensure that a widow in the church has her daily needs met (use fictitious names) in line with 1 Timothy 5.

It's Relevant!

Will your learners experience the Word of God merely as an academic discussion, to be left behind as they get back to "real life"? Or will they experience the Word as "alive and active, sharper than any double-edged sword" (Hebrews 4:12)? *Illustrate, participate, express!*

Building Relationships with Your Learners

Fostering Friendships In and Out of the Classroom

by Brett DeYoung

Most adults join an adult class to make friendships with other adults with similar interests. Use that to your advantage, both in the classroom and out. Organize your class to build friendships, and plan retreats, socials, and service projects that enrich those relationships and use them for good.

Organize for Building Friendships

Designate people who will arrive at least 15 minutes before class begins to greet class members. Ensure that each person is greeted with a warm, firm handshake and a friendly smile. Provide your members with nametags each week and enlist someone to fill out nametags for newcomers.

Providing coffee and doughnuts (or other snacks) can help the class "warm up" before the lesson is taught. Plan at least 15 to 20 minutes for informal conversation and relationship building at the beginning of a class period.

A class newsletter is a good tool for communication and relationship building on a weekly or monthly basis. It can help keep people informed about prayer requests, upcoming socials, birthdays, and anniversaries. The newsletter may include recipes, devotional thoughts, want ads from the local business community, and features from local doctors, lawyers, financial counselors, and other writers who wish to encourage others in their areas of expertise. With the influx of affordable home computer software, the newsletter can be as simple or elaborate as the class members desire. The newsletter can be given out at the end of the class session or e-mailed to members.

Decide as a class when you will contact missing class members. Enlist volunteers to contact people or families that have been absent. Follow up with phone calls, cards, and/or notes. Print special cards with sayings like, "We're praying for you," "We missed you," "Congratulations," or "Thank you." Pass the appropriate cards during class time for everyone to sign; mail them the next day.

Recruit a host or hostess for each class whose main responsibility is to watch for new people and help them feel welcome in the class. A resourceful host or hostess will introduce new people to class members who live in the same area or who have similar interests. They can also formally introduce the newcomers at the beginning of class time or during announcement time.

Encourage your class to take advantage of larger church events, such as worship, picnics, and socials. Look for class members and sit together. As the teacher, use these times to affirm and appreciate those who respond to questions during the class time.

Many times adult classes become "fishing ponds" for other ministries of the church. For instance, children's, youth, or worship departments can all benefit from volunteers from your adult class. Highlight the church's needs for volunteers on a class bulletin board or during the announcement period of the class.

Meet class members during the week for breakfast or lunch near their workplaces. Begin softball, volleyball, or other recreational activities for members and friends. Use this time to get to know each other as well as to grow in numbers.

How to Plan a Successful Retreat

Choose a location that will accomplish the goals of your retreat program. Church camps, state parks, hotels, resorts, or lodges can be great sites for a retreat. Two key factors in considering a site are cost and distance. One to two hours away is a good rule of thumb. This is far enough away to keep people from running back and forth to take care of minor details, yet not too far that cost keeps people from attending or travel limits the time for your retreat activities.

Determine the expenses of the retreat. Small churches may not have the resources or the numbers to justify the expense for their own retreats. Many colleges have campus ministries that sponsor retreats every semester. Why not take a group of young adults and join them? You could also plan area-wide retreats by combining resources with other congregations.

Look for those who have the gift of giving to share in sponsoring people who cannot attend because of financial restraints.

Look for Christian organizations that provide programs and seminars in large cities. Promise Keepers, marriage enrichment retreats, Emmaus walks, and church growth seminars are some examples. Take your class. Plan to spend extra time before and after the event to gather your group together, debrief the experience, and set personal goals for the future.

Travel, food, special speakers, entertainment, baby-sitting, publicity, lodging, and miscellaneous program costs are all items that should be considered when planning a retreat.

A retreat for young couples with young children can be enhanced if older adults in the church would adopt the children for the weekend. Another way to help with baby-sitting is to take along several high school students. They can use extra Vacation Bible School materials to conduct a separate retreat for the children.

Examine community events and the church calendar when planning a date for a retreat. Prominent local sporting events can kill a retreat that is planned on the same weekend. Each community has certain events you should always plan around. Most major holidays should be avoided unless you are trying to establish it as a family tradition among your people.

It is vitally important to communicate the nature and purpose of your retreat with the leadership of your church. When a group of people is missing on a Sunday, it can leave huge gaps to be filled by other volunteers. Planning a retreat during a major church event can leave hurt feelings on the part of both parties if not communicated well in advance.

The Five P's For Planning Effective Socials

Purpose. Ask these questions to help determine your reason for a social:

A. Are we getting this group together just to have fun?

B. Are we trying to build stronger relationships?

C. Is this an opportunity for us to reach out to our non-Christian friends?

D. Are there other adults in our church that we would like to meet and get to know?

Place. Be creative when choosing the place for the social. Don't always have your social at the church building. Experiment with traveling to each others' homes, parks, restaurants, and indoor or outdoor recreation areas.

Publicity. Use as many avenues to promote your social as possible. Most churches will allow you to write an announcement for the bulletin, newsletter, or worship service. Be creative! Film a two- to three-minute video announcing the special event. Present a short drama about meeting new people. Display posters and pictures of previous socials to stir interest.

People. Resist the temptation to have only one person plan a social. Have a small group of four to six people take different responsibilities for the five P's and recruit additional help from the class. Involving many people in the planning will result in more attending the event.

If you are targeting a college age group, socials should be planned around the holidays and other school breaks. An opportune time to minister to students can be when the church's schedule slows down during the summer months.

Program. The sky is the limit for your creativity! Decorate a room at the church to incorporate a western theme or plan a luau with a pig roast and tropical menu. Progressive dinners, mystery dinners, and cookouts are always favorites. Capitalize on Valentine's Day to bring couples together to share their wedding pictures. Ask a minister to lead the group in reaffirming their wedding vows. Follow with wedding cake and punch.

Plan a digital scavenger hunt. Divide guests into small groups and travel to a list of sites where groups must be photographed. Be sure that someone drives the course ahead of time to gauge the minimum time required. Then set a time limit, and encourage respect for local speed limits.

Sporting events can be fun. Try "volleydog"—playing volleyball and enjoying a cookout with hot dogs. Plan a tailgate cookout before a local sporting event.

Service Projects

Service projects can be as simple as cleaning up an elderly person's yard or helping to sponsor people on a short-term mission trip. Many church camps are dependent on volunteer help from local churches. Adopt a camp and then cook, landscape, clean, or build what is needed.

Many Christian adults are becoming challenged to take short-term missionary trips. Sponsor someone (or a group) who will go and lend a hand to a church-supported missionary. Or send a group to volunteer in an urban ministry, poor mountain region, or Indian reservation. Local soup kitchens and inner city missions are often in need of volunteers. Collect clothing and gifts for these families at holiday times.

Adopt a missionary family and support them financially, through prayer, and with communication. With computers and cell phones, missionaries now can communicate instantly instead of waiting weeks or months for mail delivery.

COMM_TMENT:

What Is Missing?

by Ronald G. Davis

Commitment. Church leaders search high and low for it, and too often they do not find it. Few church members today choose to make a commitment to church ministries that demand persistent presence and active participation. Could it be that few Christians are truly committed to God, to God's demands for a life of doing right? The teacher of adults should always be on the lookout for an opportunity to challenge commitment in the learners. Some simple learning activities may be a step in the right direction to "getting the *I* back into *commitment*."

How Am I Doing?

God's prophets had a primary task: to call God's wayward people back to his ways. If you are studying the prophets, consider having your class members maintain a journal during the series, a record of their own responses to the truths studied.

Make multiple copies of the following form so you can provide one to each student each week. At the end of the first week's study, introduce the concept by saying, "At the end of the week ahead, sit down and ponder how well you are doing in relationship to the commitment we have studied today. Fill in the word *Justice* (or some other key word in the first lesson) on the lines marked with an asterisk (*); then write your thoughtful responses in the other spaces."

When it comes to being committed to *_____, I rate myself a ____. [Use a scale of 1 for "barely noticeable" to 5 for "giving daily evidence."]

One occasion this week when I gave evidence I am committed to *_____ was when I _____. This event or behavior best exemplified such a commitment because it _____.

One occasion this week when my behavior or words demonstrated a lack of commitment to *_____ was when I _____.

The verse from this week's text that has the greatest impact on me is _____. The reason for this impact is _____.

Have students use the same form each week. Some key words or themes that may come up in a series on the prophets are (1) justice, (2) God's ways, (3) true worship, (4) seeking God, (5) God's requirements, (6) righteousness, (7) hope, (8) accountability, (9) trusting God, (10) hope even in pain, (11) taking responsibility, (12) returning to God, and (13) doing right. If these do not match your series, it's easy enough to replace these with your own key words.

What Is Lacking?

This weekly journaling will allow students to confront their own levels of commitment. Ask for volunteers to give candid self-assessments to the class as a whole. The problems that your students reveal may be symptoms of a deeper problem: a lack of knowledge. God's lament, through the pen of Hosea, was, "My people are destroyed from lack of knowledge" (Hosea 4:6). When disciples thoroughly know the person and will of God, commitment should be a by-product. In Simon Peter's words, "Lord, to whom shall we go? You have the words of eternal life" (John 6:68).

Consider how you can facilitate greater knowledge through memorization of pivotal verses. In the first week of the study, for example, tell your students, "I have found some significant thoughts of God in my preparation for this series of studies in the theme of commitment from God's prophets. So I have committed to learning some of those great ideas by heart." Then quote, for example, part of Amos 5:15: "Hate evil, love good; maintain justice in the courts." Offer your class an opportunity to join you in your quest to increase their own knowledge of God as found in the prophets. To this end, you can distribute commitment cards like this:

Dear God, thank you for revealing your will through your prophets. I hereby commit to learning at least ___ verses of beauty and challenge during our class's study. My prayer is that your Word will cure my lack of knowledge.

Signed _____; date _____.

Indicate that this commitment activity is strictly a personal matter and that the cards can be carried in one's Bible. Make suggestions for good verses to memorize. Regularly talking about your own progress will encourage participation.

A Context for Learning

A Good Start

by Ronald G. Davis

Classrooms should create "wide-eyed children" of learners, no matter the age. A "learning enriched environment," as educators use the term, has the potential to do so. From decorations to furnishings to a library of books, teachers want the room both to support and encourage learning. When learners walk in (or even approach), something reminds or tells them, "This is what we're studying." Some visual, aural, or other sensory stimulus helps learners recall what has been studied or piques their curiosity and interest as to what will be.

Nursery and Nativity

The Bible records the details of the births of several important characters: Isaac, Samuel, John the Baptist, and Jesus, to name a few. To create interest for such a story, set in prominent positions selected nursery furnishings: a bassinet, an infant child seat, a hanging mobile. As learners arrive, have lullaby music playing. A display of baby pictures—both of class members and of their children or grandchildren—can add "flavor" to the context.

Prepare a list of "shower" gifts that will be appropriate for the parents or baby of the featured Bible character. Either as a preview activity handed out a week before or as a session introductory activity, ask the learners to decide how each "gift" on the list is relevant to the text revelation. Consider the following lists, here given with explanatory notes.

For Samuel and his parents: an athletic shirt with the number 11 (based on Elkanah's statement that he was better to Hannah than ten sons); a razor without a blade (based on Hannah's promise that her son would never have his hair cut; anything blue (Hannah prayed for a "man child"); a "golden ear" locket (for Samuel's name means, "heard of God"); a cow (for Hannah's sacrifice at the time she gives her son to the Lord); happy face stickers (see 1 Samuel 1:18b); musical staff sheets (for Hannah to record her song of chapter 2).

For John and his parents: two senior citizen discount cards (for both parents are "well stricken in years"); a book teaching sign language (for Zechariah to use for communication during his mute period of nine months); incense (for Zechariah's duty in the temple); a book of "Names for Boys" (though the parents won't need this one); carton of soft drinks (for John will drink no "strong drink"); a five-month supply of knitting supplies (for Elisabeth's self-imposed five-month seclusion); party supplies for an "It's a boy!" celebration (see Luke 1:58); a small chalkboard and chalk (for Zechariah's use in indicating the baby's name); a big jar of honey (for John's food in the wilderness); a baby camel (for John's later clothes of camel's hair, Matthew 3:4).

For Jesus and his parents: a book on dream interpretation (though neither will need it!); engagement ring (they were "espoused"); a safe deposit box in the First Bank of Bethlehem (for safe storage of the wise men's gifts); round-trip tickets to Egypt (see Matthew 2:13-15); outdated Holiday Inn coupon (for there was "no room in the inn"); bundle of cloth strips (for the newborn); wooden folding bassinet with a straw tick (for the manger bed); a journaling notebook (for Mary to "keep and ponder" all the events); a pair of turtledoves (for the temple sacrifice at Jesus' circumcision).

Objects and Objectives

You don't have to be studying a birth story to come up with ideas for objects that can help suggest the content and goals of your lesson. Be creative with any lesson, and consider ways to apply lesson themes and to review lesson truths.

For a lesson on Job, for example, consider some of the following "context" ideas: hand out an adhesive strip to each learner arriving (to represent Job's suffering); hand out a broken piece of clay pottery (inexpensive flowerpot) to each (see Job 2:8); give each a "praying for you" card (at the end you can recommend that it be sent to someone in physical and emotional distress).

Job 38–41 could be called God's "Final Exam" for Job, an examination for which Job had no answers. For a lesson from this passage, secure a set of the traditional blue books used by schools and colleges for tests. Hand one to each person as he or she enters. Tell the class, "Number your test booklet one to twenty." Either prepare and hand out or simply present orally test questions learners will most likely be unable to answer: for example, "What is the standard deviation of the top ten batting averages of last year's American League baseball batters?" "On Moh's hardness scale, what is the number of the earth's most common mineral?" "How many kilometers is it from the earth to the nearest star?" "Translate this clause, 'God is good,' into Urdu script." "Draw a contour map of the Pacific Ocean floor." "Write the steps necessary to program a computer to do a spell check in a language not using the English alphabet." and other such "impossible" questions. After only four or five, the point will be obvious. Launch into the text.

For a lesson from Ecclesiastes 3, collect and display a variety of clocks. Label each clock with a daily activity of necessity and/or importance. Such items as "brushing teeth," "putting shoes on," "praying," "Bible reading," "eating," "sleeping," "helping someone," and others can be included. Make the labels large enough to be legible across the room. Begin by saying, "Each day there are some things that we just don't have time for." Select a clock, read the label aloud, and put the clock conspicuously in the wastebasket. Put some of the "necessary" items in first. At some point say, "What makes a daily activity 'necessary'?"

For a lesson on Ecclesiastes 12 (or any text with an exhortation to remember), have someone tie a loose bow of ribbon or string around a finger of each arriving student. When all are in and seated, ask all to hold up their hands with the bows and ask, "Now what was that you were supposed to remember?"

A lesson from the Song of Solomon easily lends itself to decorating the room with valentines or simple cut-out hearts. A lesson from Esther 8 and 9 includes the origin of the Jewish celebration of Purim, the survival of the Jews in Persia. This or some other lesson with a celebration theme could be enhanced with party decorations, such as balloons and streamers.

The teacher with insight into how adults learn will look each week for ways to reflect content and objectives in the very space where study will occur. Will learners come into a sterile, nondescript room? Or will they enter an "enriched learning environment"? The teacher decides.

DEALING WITH DIFFICULT STUDENTS

Problem Behavior in the Adult Classroom

by James Riley Estep, Jr.

"I thought we were talking about adults! What do you mean difficult students? Adults aren't text-messaging, trash-talking, disrespectful teens and tweens!" Reality check: difficult students exist in learning environments at all age levels. While adults may not be running around the room or overtly and intentionally misbehaving, nevertheless they can be a distraction.

Generally speaking, there are five types of difficult students you may encounter in adult classrooms. Deciding what approach to take in dealing with a difficult student first involves a diagnosis of which problem-type is presenting itself.

The Know-It-All

The Know-It-All uses the class setting of the Sunday school hour to demonstrate his or her "superior" knowledge and understanding of the subject. The Know-It-All often appears to be in competition with the teacher. Know-It-Alls may feel the need to comment on every statement made by the teacher, add "deeper" insights to the lesson, or (at worst) directly oppose the teacher's ideas. A Know-It-All may try to set himself or herself up as the definitive voice of truth for the class. This becomes a distraction to other learners as it tends to change the class discussion or lecture into a debate.

There are several options for handling this type of difficult student. One method is to design your class with a time designated intentionally for discussion, particularly in small groups. This may limit the Know-It-All's opportunities to interrupt.

Another tactic is to recruit this kind of student to be a teacher. However, some Know-It-Alls will not accept the call to teach. They may prefer to snipe at the teacher rather than assume the teaching role itself—a role that would put the Know-It-All in a vulnerable position of being on the receiving end of the sniping!

A third tactic is to deal directly with the real issue of the Know-It-All's character flaw with a gentle, one-on-one confrontation. This involves a spiritually mature person taking the Know-It-All aside outside of class and asking, "Do you realize what you're doing in the classroom?" The resulting discussion can be very productive if the confronter is skilled at dealing with defensive reactions that may pop up.

Caution: it is usually not wise for you, the teacher, to try to neutralize the Know-It-All by countering his or her "deeper" insights with "even deeper yet" insights of your own. This tactic can deteriorate quickly into a tawdry game of one-upmanship.

The Grumbler

The Grumbler uses your classroom as a platform for expressing complaints. Regardless of the topic being discussed, the Grumbler is able to turn it into an occasion for a negative remark about the congregation, the minister, or Christianity in general.

You the teacher must realize that this is a spiritual matter that originates beyond the walls of your Sunday school classroom. The Grumbler is obviously feeling some kind of pain, has unresolved issues, or has been hurt by someone. Dealing with a Grumbler requires a pastoral approach.

Hence, the best way to deal with a Grumbler is outside the class, one-on-one. That meeting does not necessarily have to include you, the teacher, but it should involve a respected leader of your congregation. Such a meeting will try to pinpoint the specific issues with which the Grumbler has concerns.

Taking an open, non-defensive posture toward Grumblers is often helpful in getting them to open up and share concerns. Many times they simply want to be heard. The fact that someone is taking time to listen to the Grumbler affirms that his or her concerns are being heard. The Grumbler needs to be made aware, however, that he or she should take the concerns directly to the church leadership rather than to your class.

The Light-Shiner

Light-Shiners use the classroom to show how they exemplify the points of the lesson. They set themselves up as a paradigm for the Christian life and tend to interpret the Scriptures in terms of their personal lifestyle. For example, when hearing a lesson on giving to the poor, Light-Shiners feel compelled to tell the class about their involvement with the homeless, how much they've given to groups such as the Salvation Army, etc. As a result, class members become annoyed by the self-promoting personal testimonial that occurs in every class session.

One method of dealing with the Light-Shiner is to ensure that all your learners have opportunity to share how they demonstrate the topic of the day in their lives. You can do this by asking each student, one by one, to identify how he or she practices the biblical principle at hand. In this way you end up making the Light-Shiner one candle among many rather than the solitary light.

Light-Shiners need to balance Matthew 5:14-16 with Matthew 6:1-4; thus a lesson in that regard may be in order. If they can understand that the focus is not to be on themselves, Light-Shiners can become wonderful mentors.

The Café-Goer

I have an affinity for coffee and fellowship! But I also realize that Sunday school is more than coffee and coffee talk. I enjoy my time at the local coffeehouse and the opportunity it brings for discussion and even spiritual support. But I also know that Sunday school classrooms are not coffeehouses.

However, Café-Goers don't share this awareness. They spend an inordinate time around the class coffeepot conversing with friends, and they may have to be reminded more than once "It's time to start the lesson." Even then they may continue chatting throughout the lesson (typically about anything but the lesson topic).

One tactic to deal with the Café-Goer is to voice a gentle hint such as, "I see some discussions going on—am I way off course on this? Questions, comments, concerns?" This should draw everyone's attention back to the topic under discussion.

Café-Goers often are simply unaware of the distractions they are causing. They may view Sunday school primarily as an opportunity for fellowship rather than as a teaching venue. A gentle hint as suggested may be all that is needed.

The High-Maintenance Individual

Do you have folks in your class who are always expressing personal issues for prayer requests, identifying themselves as examples of misfortune, or even openly crying in class? If so, you may have High-Maintenance Individuals on your hands. These are people who always seem to be in a state of spiritual or personal crisis.

Such folks need intentional pastoral support. A primary function of the church is to provide such support, of course. But an adult Sunday school classroom usually is not the best place to provide it. Yes, the church exists to help troubled souls. But to allow your classroom to become a crisis-counseling center is to change the design of the Sunday school hour into something other than a Bible-teaching venue.

None of this is meant to be insensitive to the genuine needs of people in crisis. Members of your Sunday school class can indeed serve as crisis counselors and crisis responders in times of death, spiritual doubt, financial problems, etc. These are normal and expected ministries of class members with one another. But that is not to say that the Sunday school hour is the best time for such ministries to occur.

The key response in such cases is *referral*. A person going through crisis often needs more and different help than is available during the Sunday school hour. Make arrangements for your troubled individuals to get counseling from an appropriate source, such as your minister, an elder, or Christian counselor. Referral addresses the issues of the troubled individual in the best way possible while helping minimize the chance that your Sunday school hour will become something it is not designed to be.

Why This Is Important

As you read the five descriptions above, images of certain individuals probably entered your mind. (Maybe you even saw yourself!) Teachers cannot avoid difficult students; it is part of the call to the teaching ministry.

Remember: your goal as teacher is to keep your lesson aims at the center as you teach the Word and help your students apply it. The behavior of difficult students takes you away from this goal. In effect, such behavior, if left unchecked, will change the purpose of the class. The more mature members of the class realize their responsibility to the class as a whole. Difficult students, by contrast, use the classroom as a means of fulfilling a personal agenda, either intentionally or unintentionally.

Many teachers simply tolerate the behavior of difficult students. *This is not really an option*, since such behaviors are counterproductive to a learning environment and actually may do harm to other students. Newcomers to the class may end up with a poor experience and may choose not to return as a result. In short, the teacher *must* deal with difficult students. The problem will rarely correct itself if ignored. Recognizing the problem is the first step toward fixing it.

The Drama of the Gospel

Using Drama in the Adult Classroom

by Ronald G. Davis

The grand truths expressed by Paul in the epistles to the Romans and Galatians is high drama. The conflict is nothing less than good versus evil, sin versus righteousness, life versus death, law versus grace.

The "cast" finds its villain in anyone who would work on behalf of the chief villain, Satan. Sometimes it is the Judaizers, who want to undermine and destroy Paul's work. Other times it is the Siren Sin that lures even the apostle.

The stage is as broad as the Roman empire, and the backdrops picture both the rural and isolated towns of Galatia and the urban sprawl and decadence of Rome itself.

The protagonist is in reality Christ himself, but Paul and the local Christians represent him in face-to-face confrontation with the antagonist. Climax of the drama comes at the cross, where the resolution of the conflict is realized and complete. Goodness, righteousness, life, grace—all are made clear and demonstrated to be victorious.

To emphasize the dramatic nature of the Bible study material, especially in Romans and Galatians, and to utilize a common interest of adults, learning activities involving drama can be good choices. Dramatic interviews, pantomimes, skits, and role plays offer useful techniques for studying biblical truths.

Dramatic Interviews

A dramatic interview, a supposed face-to-face with a biblical person or a representative of a biblical group, lends itself to learner involvement in nonthreatening ways. The apostle Paul, a Christian named in Romans 16, a soldier who was assigned to "guard" Paul in his Roman prison later, or a Jewish legalist from Galatia—all could be worthy interviewees. Significant questions could be asked from both the biblical text and the historical/geographical setting.

Let's interview a Jewish legalist from Galatia, "A. Lawson Lauze," as an introduction to a series of lessons from Galatians. Consider such questions as these:

- Mr. Lauze, what specifically is it that you are unhappy about in Paul's preaching?
- Well, Lawson, what is your strategy for contradicting the gospel of grace?
- Did you come from Jerusalem to Galatia to speak for the law? Did someone send you?
- What kind of success, brother Lauze, are you and your friends having in Galatia?
- How did the decree of the Jerusalem church (Acts 15:23-29) affect your plan?
- When Paul's letter arrived in Galatia, how did you feel? How did you respond?
- How did the Galatian Christians respond to Paul's letter? And how did they react to you and your friends then?
- What will it take to get you to see Paul's presentation of the gospel of justification by grace?

The person playing Mr. Lauze needs to be recruited early and prepared for his responses. A careful reading of the whole epistle plus a study of the problem of the Judaizers will be essential. The teacher can do the interview himself, or he can invite the class to ask the questions he assigns or ones of their own creativity and composition. A discussion of the responses made is critical to gaining full value.

Pantomimes

Some texts lend themselves to pantomime as a way to draw the learners' attention. Pantomime, of course, implies that with a few broad strokes of wordless movement, observers can recognize what is happening. If the pantomimes are tied to a particular text, the task becomes even easier, a simple case of "matching."

Romans 14:1-13 provides a good example of such a possibility. Recruit class members to pantomime each of the following verse representations. (As you begin, you may want to do the first one yourself to show what is expected.) Tell your class to open their Bibles to the text, skim through it, and be ready to identify any verse(s) represented in a pantomime.

1. (One player.) The player goes to a calendar on the wall, puts his finger on a day, looks surprised, then falls to his knees in a prayerful attitude (vv. 5, 6).

2. (Two players.) One player is sitting on a park bench (two chairs) and idly tossing food to birds; the second one is ambling toward the first holding a large book open in front of him and engrossed by it. The sitter sees the walker coming, picks up a large, heavy rock and places it in the walker's path. The walker arrives, stumbles, and falls (v. 13).

3. (One player.) The player sits at a desk writing furiously into a book very clearly labeled "My Diary." After a brief time, he slams the book shut, stands, and lifts his eyes and the book heavenward (v. 12).

Skits

Skits are fully delineated mini-dramas, often humorous, designed to introduce a key truth to be studied or to repeat and reinforce one just immediately past. The script for a skit may be bare bones, but it is complete (in contrast to role plays to be discussed below).

Romans 12:19 includes the injunction "Do not take revenge." For a lesson from this chapter, consider this skit for two players, husband and wife:

The husband sits in his easy chair holding a legal pad with a list of large-print entries. As he twiddles his pen and stares, his wife enters.

Wife: Dave, what in the world has your attention so focused?

(He turns the pad toward his wife.)

Wife: What is that a list of? It doesn't look very kind.

Husband: Kind? I don't want it to be kind. I told you what Steve did to me at work. He made me look like an idiot in front of Mr. Marsh. This is my "Get-even" list.

Wife: Oh, it's your "Even-Steven" list? (sarcastically)

Husband: Hey, I like that! Let me write that at the top.

Wife: I wasn't trying to encourage you, Dave. That doesn't sound Christian at all.

Husband: Christian? That was not my intention. Some behaviors have to be met head on—an eye for an eye, you might say.

Wife: It sounds as if you're letting your I—that's a capital one (with her index finger she draws a capital I in the air in front of Dave's face)—keep you from seeing what you're doing.

Husband: Well, sometimes a man just has to stand up for himself.

Wife: (picks up a Bible, opens it, and hands it to him) Look at Romans 12:19. I guess you can make things right better than God can, huh? Wear a mask to work tomorrow; call yourself "The Masked Avenger." Just don't call yourself a Christian.

Most classes have one or more class members who would enjoy the challenge of writing such skits on a verse or on a lesson theme.

Role Plays

Role play, sometimes called sociodrama, involves actors in a situation of conflict and undetermined resolution, designed to mimic everyday life without the consequences. The players are given initial notes as to the situation (a "jumping off" point) and brief descriptions of their individual characters, but the dialogue and direction are left to their spontaneous choices. Role play is designed to elicit discussion from the observers, so a role play cannot be done incorrectly.

Consider the following role play for a lesson on Romans 1:1-17, having to do with Paul's readiness to present the gospel in all places on every opportunity.

A mother is gathering her husband, teenage daughter, and ten-year-old son to carry a full meal to the house next door. New neighbors of Latin American heritage just moved in the day before, and she wants to take supper to that family. The family in this role play is a faithful, church-going family. As the mother gathers her family and starts handing the food to each, she asks, "Now what do we want to talk about and not talk about?" One family member will ask, "Are we going to invite them to church?"

The teacher will need five copies of the situation: one for each player, and one for himself. As the four players meet very briefly to prepare (but not to reveal their own specific plan to each other), the teacher can describe the occasion and introduce the players.

Once the family "walks out the door, headed for the neighbor's house," the teacher can ask the class such questions as, "Did the family make the right decisions?" "Are their decisions realistic or idealistic?" "What different attitudes did you sense?" "What is there in today's text that is relevant to such a beginning relationship?"

An effective role play may well be worthy of repeating, letting new players (or the same ones) change the scenario as they go.

Theatre, as a context for presenting truth and wisdom or falsehood and folly, is as old as urbanized civilization. Manuscripts of dramas and remains of ancient theatre structures have filled the shovels of archaeologists. From the dramatic play of small children to the common adult attendance at movies, stage plays, and television, people are drawn to drama. Any way that the teacher can use that inclination will sharpen the adult learners' focus and enhance their understanding.

EFFECTIVE CHRISTIANS
Doctrine = Practice

by Ronald G. Davis

If God's project is effective Christians, what exactly is it that makes a Christian effective? What is needed is the very same thing anyone with any responsibility needs: ability to make the responses necessary to accomplish the task! That is, a person can do what is needed to fulfill his or her purpose. What, then, is it that the Christian needs to do? To be built up (along with fellow Christians) in strength of faith; to worship and praise the Lord; to announce the good news of salvation to all who will listen. He or she has the same purposes as does the church: edification, fellowship, worship, and evangelism. The epistle Paul wrote to the Roman Christians of the first century carry the same Spirit-filled power and necessity to us twenty-first-century Christians.

The Core of Effectiveness

At the core of Christian effectiveness is a working knowledge of the Word of God. And few books of the Bible offer the practical power of Romans. Certainly in the study of this epistle, the teacher will want to encourage and facilitate a deep, usable knowledge of the grand truths studied. Bible memorization must be at the forefront of strategies used.

A key verse in each lesson text will reveal some of those grand truths. (Your curriculum may designate such a verse in each lesson, or you may select a verse of your own choosing.) Consider having a learner with an effective voice record every key verse (with reference) for your unit of study and burn CDs for distribution to all class members. (Note: *The King James Version* is free of copyright restrictions; other versions will require permission.) When these are distributed, announce the intention and suggest that learners fill their opportune times—driving, cooking, washing dishes, resting—listening to these verses repeatedly.

Since not everyone in your class is an auditory learner, consider handing out a one-a-day worksheet for a selected key verse of each week with seven different activities to be used one a day. The worksheet might resemble the following, if Romans 1:16 were your key verse, with the direction to tear off each day as it is completed:

Sunday—"For I am not _____ of the _____, because it is the _____ of God that brings _____ to everyone who _____."

Monday—"Rof I am ton aadehms of the eglops, abceesu it is the eoprw of God that brings aailonstv to eeeonrvy who beeeilsv."

Tuesday—am ashamed because believes brings everyone for God gospel I is it not of of power salvation that the the to who.

Wednesday—Gps J bn opu btibnfe pg uif hptqfm cfdbvtf ju jt uif qpxfs pg Hpe uibu csjoht tbmwbujpo up fwfszpof xip cfmjfwft.

Thursday*—IRU J CO QRW HZOHTLK QH WKH MUYVKR ILJHBZL KV KU WKH UTBJW QH JRG XLEX HWOTMY BJUEJCRXW VQ MDMZGWVM ZKR JMTQM-DMA.

Friday—"For __   __ __   __ __ __   __ __ __ __ __ __ __   __ __   __ __ __ __ __ __ __ __ __, because __ __   __ __   __ __ __   __ __ __ __ __ __   __ __   __ __ __ that __ __ __ __ __ __   __ __ __ __ __ __ __ __ __ __ to __ __ __ __ __ __ __ __   __ __ __ __ __ __ __ __ __ __."

Saturday—Quote Romans 1:16.

Many learners find that memorization and melody go hand in hand. Who can resist a snappy jingle? (In fact, who can get one out of his or her head?) Probably in your group of learners there are some who would find joy in developing a singable tune for selected verses from your unit of study. Early in the study (or previous to its start), seek volunteers to compose a simple tune for verses you identify as important. For example, from Romans 2, "God does not show favoritism" (v. 11); from Romans 5, "Since we have been justified through faith, we have peace with God through our Lord Jesus Christ" (v. 1). Of course, the writer could add or alter words slightly to develop a singable chorus; for example, Romans 2:11 could be effective as:

There is no favoritism with God;

There is no favoritism with God;

There is no favoritism with God,

So why is there prejudice in us?

[*Solution for Thursday: move up in the alphabet by the number of letters in any given word.]

The Fabric of the Gospel

Though we tend to separate doctrinal and practical elements of the gospel, someone has rightly said, "There is nothing more practical than solid doctrine, and there is nothing more doctrinal than sound practice." Paul's "woven" version of the gospel, with doctrine as the foundation and practice as the structure, is a marvel of design—God's design.

For a session and text of your choice develop a front-and-back sheet of Doctrine and Practical Application pairs. Print the sheet so that the related practice is on the reverse of the doctrinal truth. Put about ten pairs on the sheet, cut them apart for the activity described below.

As a sample, consider a lesson from Galatians 1:1-12. Here are possible doctrine and practice "pairs": (1) Our Lord Jesus Christ will deliver us from this present evil world (v. 4), and "As I read the bad news in the newspaper or watch it on television, I can praise the Lord that he will take me away from all the wickedness." (2) God the Father raised Jesus from the dead (v. 1), and "I can remain joyful when I attend the funeral of a godly friend or family member." (3) Perverted forms of the gospel have existed since the first century (v. 7), and "I must examine every presentation of the gospel—from religious television to popular media—for accuracy to the Word of Christ." (4) The pure gospel is that preached by Paul and the apostles in the first century (vv. 8, 9), and "My study of the Gospels and the book of Acts and the epistles is the safest way to learn the gospel." (5) Being a servant of Christ, I will not necessarily please many (v. 10), and "I must be willing to part with friends and even family to be Jesus' disciple, if it comes to a choice" (see Luke 14:26). (6) The good news of the gospel is not man-made truth, but revelation from God (vv. 11, 12), and "I must reject all explanations of truth that are of purely human origin and speculation." (7) There is a curse on the one who distorts or rejects the gospel of Christ (vv. 8, 9), and "I must work to correct and edify anyone whom I find distorting the gospel, to save that person from God's curse." (8) The heart of the gospel is the grace of Christ (v. 6), and "I have no anxiety about being good enough for God, for I am saved by grace."

When class members arrive, hand each a rectangular piece carrying one of the doctrinal truth/practical application pairs. (Duplicate the sheet if you have more than eight class members.) Direct them to look at only one side. When you come to the application segment of your lesson, say, "Your task is to decide what should be on the other side of your sheet—if you see a doctrine (with verse reference), what is the practical application? If you see a practical application, what doctrine (and verse[s]) is relevant?" Let group members share some of their statements and their decisions for the reverse, and then let them read both sides. Of course, their speculative decisions need not match the statements and references given. Discuss the differences when they are seen.

Into Life

The epistles were designed by God to challenge Christians to be true to the doctrine they have been taught. Doctrine is true whether individuals apply it to life or not, but the only personal value that doctrine has is seen in daily application. There is the "What's So" of the gospel, but there is also the "So What?"

With every lesson, the wise teacher realizes his study and plan are incomplete until he asks, "So what? What is there about today's truths that can make a difference in the life of my learners this week?"

Teach your students to read the epistles with a "So What?" attitude—that is, to ponder the personal consequences of each truth revealed. Consider dividing your class into two groups for reading the texts antiphonally one or more weeks of the study: one group to read a verse, and the second group to exclaim, "So What!" after each. Be certain to explain that this is in no way questioning the validity of the text, but is a simple challenge to consider the text personally and behaviorally.

Teaching the facts of doctrine is never an end of itself. We much teach our students to "do." But we cannot do what we do not know. The wise teacher of adults—like Paul—combines truth with application.

THE END

Making Sure It Is Right

by Ronald G. Davis

Jesus said, "I am the Alpha and the Omega," the "Beginning and the End" (Revelation 1:8; 22:13). When he is allowed to be that in the individual disciple's life, the ultimate end definitely will be right.

Teachers naturally want their lessons to lead toward that good end. Yet the difference that a brief study of a Bible text makes in the life of a student is difficult to judge. Too often Bible teachers think that their task stops at explanation of text and context. Too often teachers are so rushed to "cover it all" that they ignore the end, the application step. Though Scriptures certainly are not obscure in their implications for life, most adults could use some encouragement and direction for the *So what?* stage of learning. The teacher's job is to help students see the truth's implications for life and point them to action. The teacher fulfills this responsibility with *reminders and reinforcers* and with a *call to action*.

Reminders and Reinforcers

Curriculum for children often includes take-home items. These are either products the children have produced in a learning activity or items the teacher or curriculum publisher have produced to correlate with truths studied. These are designed to give the learner "one more look" at the ideas (reminder) and/or an opportunity to communicate the lesson learned to someone else (reinforcement). The same learning concept holds true for adults: one more look—even a momentary notice—and an opportunity to share an idea learned with another person are valuable.

For example, the overriding emphasis in 1 John is *love*. During a study of 1 John, a constant reminder of love can take the form of a sticker, badge, or pin with a heart illustration to be worn week-to-week. This can, in turn, become the occasion for answering the likely inquiry, "Why are you wearing that heart?"

For the series that focuses on the resurrection, a teacher can encourage the learners to wear an emblem of Jesus' death and resurrection. This would announce with godly pride, "I am a Christian. I have a living hope of resurrection and eternal life!" Suggest a simple *ET* badge to get attention.

Curiosity can be answered, "It means *Empty Tomb*!" One can then explain that Jesus is the only true "extraterrestrial"; he is the only one to come to earth from Heaven, then go "back home" to prepare for his friends' arrival.

Studies that deal with the end times and the glories of the new heaven and new earth call for simple "earth stickers." Wearing these creates the chance for remembering and revealing to others our hope: new earth and new Heaven. Some celebrate Earth Day on April 22 each year; your stickers can suggest a New Earth Day to anticipate Jesus' return.

You can also make it easy for your learners to carry a copy of the Bible texts with them day to day. This will encourage a more-than-once look at God's Word. Passages from your lesson texts can be legibly copied onto the front and back of two or three sheets of paper. A suggestion to keep them handy at one's work station for examination during breaks or lunch may create a habit of regular Bible reading.

Call to Action

The Bible's *call to action* deals with both internal character and external deeds. Though righteousness (internal integrity) and righteous deeds (benevolent acts of kindness and faith) cannot truly be separated, some lesson texts emphasize one, some the other. As the apostle John notes, "This is how we know who the children of God are: . . . Anyone who does not do what is right is not God's child" (1 John 3:10). No righteous deeds, no character of true righteousness!

Consider, for example, 1 John 3:17. There the apostle says bluntly, "If anyone has material possessions and sees a brother or sister in need but has no pity on them, how can the love of God be in that person?" You can use this text as opportunity for the class to make a collection and distribution to the needy. Try collecting gloves and mittens for the homeless, collecting money for one month's rent for a needy family, or initiating a drive for canned meat for the church's food pantry.

Calls to action can be presented in other ways as well. Many New Testament texts reveal God's standards for godly living, and when a disciple confronts them, he or she cannot but ask, "How am I doing?" Prime tasks of the teacher are to make sure the mirror of the Word is crystal clear and that it is squarely faced by every student. One strategy the teacher has in this regard is to present learners a "rating scale" to elicit a self-evaluation. The goal is to highlight needed improvements in one's character and thought life.

Consider, for example, Revelation 4, as it pictures worship at the throne in Heaven. Who doesn't need to ponder a personal response to such statements as "I have proper fear and reverence for God"; "My understanding of God's holiness keeps me from choosing the unholy"; "I fully appreciate the concept of God's eternal nature"; "I believe that God created all things, and so I thank him for all that is"; "I will not withhold anything that I have from my worship of God"; and "I think about Heaven and its glories." Encouraging learners to choose *Always, Often, Sometimes,* or *Never* as responses will force a consideration of "What do I need to do now?"

A teacher also can offer simple fill-in-and-sign statements to challenge students to meet the Spirit's standards. Revelation 7 and its picture of the saved at the throne of God could be accompanied by statements such as *I, _____, want to wear the white robe of the saved; I, _____, want to be sheltered by God's tent of love; I, _____, want to know the comfort of Heaven's satisfying provisions; I, _____, want to walk with the Lamb to the springs of living water.*

Action must include prayer, of course. This is one of the absolutely essential Christian disciplines. So the good teacher is always looking for ways to encourage prayer related to texts studied. Some of those prayers will be pure praise and thanksgiving to the worthy God.

Revelation 19 includes a call to God's people to praise him (v. 5). A seven-day prayer stimulus card, distributed to each person as he or she leaves class, can encourage remembrance of the study and a need to put those truths to work in life. Consider the following, based on Revelation 19:1-10:

Monday: Thank God for making things right (v. 2).

Tuesday: Sing *hallelujah* because the Lord our God Almighty reigns (v. 6).

Wednesday: Humbly honor the Lord for allowing you to wear the fine linen of righteous deeds (vv. 7, 8).

Thursday: Express your joy at receiving an invitation to the marriage supper of the Lamb (v. 9).

Friday: Affirm your confident belief that the words of God are true and that you are privileged to hear and know them (v. 9b).

Saturday: Thank God for the company of believers with whom you worship (v. 10a).

Sunday: Put feet on your prayer as you go to a place of worship today to worship God and him only (v. 10b).

Praise is not the only way to pray, of course. Prayers of repentance and petition are also needed. For all adults there are "shadow moments" in which one's behavior is not fully characterized by love. First John 2:7-17 challenges every Christian to live in the light of love. Our shortfalls here call for heartfelt prayers of repentance and petition for God's help.

Though ultimately the teacher wants the students to word their own prayers, suggesting some prayers may be a step in that direction. For a lesson on the text from 1 John 2 cited above, offer this prayer: "Father who loves me, help me to be like you. When I am drawn to love the world and things in it, draw me back to you. By your indwelling Spirit push aside my cravings, lusts, and boastings. Help me to know and do your will; I want to live forever. In Jesus' name, amen." Occasionally asking students simply to echo sincerely a prayer of yours will be effective.

The End

The end of every Bible study occurs after the study is over: in the daily life of each student. A concerned teacher of adults knows that and does what he or she can do to see that truths are carried from the place of study to the place of life and service. Only then does Jesus—the beginning and the end—have a true disciple.

Expanding Your Preparation
Using Internet Resources

by Eleanor A. Daniel

Many teachers long for added resources to guide them in their study and preparation for teaching adults. Their personal resources have limitations, some more than others. Some do not live near a library that offers much in the way of biblical study resources.

But these limitations need not be a hindrance to effective preparation to teach—not in this day and age—if you have access to the Internet. Imagine expanding your resources exponentially! You can do it with the resources at your fingertips via the Internet.

[Special note: the listing of Internet sites in this article is not necessarily an endorsement of everything to be found on those sites. Some sites undoubtedly have been created by those who hold very different doctrinal convictions from your own. The watchword is "use discretion"!]

Resources for Nearly Any Lesson

Don't have a concordance? Not to worry, just go to www.biblegateway.com. This resource will allow you to search for key words and topics. It has a wide range of Bible versions and can display different versions in parallel columns. Another Bible site is www.blueletterbible.org. This site has several Bible versions as well as commentaries and other study tools. You can even search *Strong's Concordance* and see which Greek or Hebrew word is behind any word in the translation. Want to know what hymn or famous work of art was inspired by a particular Bible verse? This is the place to go to find that out too!

Another helpful resource is www.answers.com. This site provides information for a variety of areas, not just religious studies. When you arrive at the page, click on the "Reference Library," where one of the choices is Religion & Spirituality. This section features, among other things, a Bible dictionary as well as comparative readings of Bible texts.

A third resource is www.bible-history.com. A long list of categories appears on the left side of the screen. Some of these may aid your preparation. This site also includes a number of church history resources. A fourth general resource is the Resource Pages for Biblical Studies that is found at www.torreys.org/bible. Here you can find pages that examine texts and translations, electronic publications, and material relating to the social aspects of the Mediterranean world.

Another source with a great many helps is www.Biblestudytools.com. This site, like Biblegateway, contains several Bible translations. It also has Bible commentaries, encyclopedias, dictionaries, a parallel Bible, and interlinear Bible. Under the search window, in which you can type a topic or subject, you'll find tabs for Bibles, references, Bible study, and pastors. The references tab opens up a wealth of resources including the works of Josephus. For a usually reliable (though not inspired) history of the Jews from the first century, Josephus's works are a wonderful resource.

Archaeological evidence and background for biblical lessons can be found at www.biblehistory .net. This site has two tabs, "Read Book 1" and "Read Book 2" that contain lists (and links) to a number of articles that may prove useful in lesson preparation. Clicking on one of these links will begin a download of a file to your computer (a "pdf") that you can save and use as a handout or simply read in preparation for the lesson. For example, www.biblehistory.net/Joshua.pdf gives some interesting details about a letter that archaeologists have discovered, a letter that was sent from Jerusalem to Egypt asking for help against the "Habiru," probably the "Hebrews" whom Joshua was leading in the conquest of the land of Canaan.

For Old Testament studies, some Jewish resources can be helpful. One such site is www.jewish encyclopedia.com, which provides the entire text of the 1906 print edition of the Jewish Encyclopedia online. Topics can be found instantly by typing the word, *Rahab* for example, (with quotation marks) in the search window. This not only gets you the article on Rahab, but every other mention of *Rahab* in other articles as well.

The site www.newadvent.org is an online Catholic encyclopedia. Click on a letter of the alphabet just below the header to get a list of topics that begin with that letter. If you just don't know where to look, the site www.gotquestions.org might be useful. Just type your question in the search box.

General search engines can also provide help. Probably everyone knows of Google (www .google.com), but there are others, such as Bing (www.bing.com), Yahoo (www.yahoo.com) and Ask (www.ask.com). There are others, but space does not allow a full listing.

Helps for Lessons from the Uniform Series

Standard Publishing has two Web sites that you will find helpful. To gain access to articles and essays in *The Lookout* magazine, go to www.lookoutmag.com. There you will find three weekly columns that are of great help to anyone teaching lessons from the Uniform Series: "This Week with the Word," "The Lesson and Life," and "Where You Live." These features provide brief notes on the lesson text, application of the text to life, and some poignant questions to engage a small group discussion of the text.

Another resource from Standard Publishing is a treatment of the lesson each week at www. christianstandard.com, which is the home page of *Christian Standard* magazine. One of the topics on the menu is "Sunday School Lesson," which features an essay that develops the lesson, again from the Uniform Series, for the week. Other publishers of Uniform Lesson material have their own web sites, and much can be gleaned from these sources as well. Again, space does not allow a full listing of such sites. But if you are using the Uniform Series, your printed material will almost certainly include a URL (the web address) for the publisher.

Sites Providing Helps for Presentation

Publishers are increasingly adding digital media to the printed curriculum. Videos, audios, and PowerPoint presentations are becoming common supplements. You can find additional presentation helps online. Here are three potential sites to assist you:

www.bibleteachingnotes.com
www.bible.org/index.php
www.mintools.com/teaching-ministry.htm

These resources are not tied to any specific lesson or topic. They will provide continuing help to enhance your teaching.

Criteria for Selecting Internet Resources

Just as every book on a topic in a library is not necessarily useful for every purpose, the same is true of Internet resources. Also remember that Internet resources can be posted far more easily than books can be published, making it possible for anyone to distribute any notion or falsehood via the Internet easily. So be selective in what you use. Here are a few guidelines:

• Make sure to explore general resources (such as those listed in the first section above). Tried and true Bible dictionaries, maps, and treatments of history such as those at Bible Gateway will generally serve you well.

• Treatments of texts such as those found on *The Lookout* and *Christian Standard* sites are also good places to begin. These are not exhaustive treatments of the text, to be sure, but they provide a tone and direction that can serve as a helpful comparison with other material you find.

• When you find unfamiliar ideas and theories, see how those square with accepted resources. If they disagree, search a bit more to see if you find the unfamiliar view critiqued by other sites.

• Information from Web sites by biblical studies professors at reputable colleges and seminaries often are good to use for comparison with ideas acquired from other, lesser known sites.

• Discuss your findings—especially those of which you are uncertain—with your minister or another knowledgeable Bible teacher in your congregation.

Even after you've had opportunity to determine the worth of the material, it's still vital to "be selective." In fact, it is only after you have done your evaluation of a site's material are you equipped to be selective.

Conclusion

Internet resources expand your opportunities for study and presentation of Bible lessons. The Internet provides a library at your fingertips. But one additional caution is in order: *There are no shortcuts to good preparation.*

Internet sites, as much information as they may give you, cannot prepare for you. You have to search-and-read, assess the validity of the information, assemble (and sometimes discard) that information, and weave what is useful and relevant into your presentation. A web site cannot determine the key idea you will emphasize in the lesson. Nor can it shape the outline or choose the teaching methods and illustrations. A big pile of information left unorganized is just that.

In other words, you still have to do the hard work of preparation if you want to teach effectively. But if you use your expanded study possibilities wisely and prepare well, you will enjoy the fruits of your labor as you present effective Bible lessons.

GOING AROUND DOING GOOD

Teaching With Projects

by Ronald G. Davis

Learning Bible content is never intended to be an end in itself. Notable atheists and agnostics have shown skill in quoting Scripture, but their knowledge of God's Word has not accomplished what it can do and is designed to do. Ephesians 4:11, 12 says the gifts given to the church are meant to prepare disciples for works of service. Every believer should closely resemble the Master, who is characterized as one who "went around doing good" (Acts 10:38).

Any study from the Gospels is going to focus on certain actions done by Jesus—particularly his miracles. And while there is an emphasis on the divine power in Jesus' deeds, we must note also the motive. The Lord's deeds are done out of a heart of compassion. From calming the disciples' terror on the sea to rolling back the depressing weight of parental anxiety of Jairus for his daughter, Jesus acted because he loved those for whom he did his marvelous acts. He went around doing good because he is good. So must be his disciples.

In addition to the knowledge and belief objectives every adult teacher has for his learners, he certainly will have basic behavior objectives. What good is knowledge unless it builds faith? What good is faith if it does not issue forth in good deeds of service?

Plans and Projects

Teachers want results. Teaching by projects is a logical culmination of wanting results. Projects can be designed for learning groups (the whole class or small groups within the class) or individuals. Some can be accomplished in the classroom; some require learners to leave the classroom with intentions—intentions to do good. Some require presents, tangible evidence of loving grace; some require presence, simply "being there." Some are long-term and time-consuming; some are "along-the-way" interludes.

In any lesson series, the perceptive teacher will ask, "What can I have my learners do—or at least recommend they do—that will demonstrate they are learning the truths of our texts?"

Fear and Faith

A number of Gospel texts picture Jesus at work allaying the fears and anxieties of people in physical and emotional distress. Consider the healing of the synagogue ruler's daughter (Matthew 9:18-26; Mark 5:22-43; Luke 8:40-56). Consider Jesus' dealing with the desperate Syrophoenician mother in Matthew 15:21-28; Mark 7:24-30. What deeds of kindness can be done for parents who are struggling with the panic and disruption of an ailing child? Will something as simple as addressing a "Thinking of You" card from the whole class be of value? Will such occasions demand that the class consider a system of once-a-week child-care provision to enable parents a time of personal respite? Will a monetary gift from the class (or simply a wholesome game or toy for a child) prove to be an encouraging act of worth? Does the church need a support group for parents in such circumstances, and how can an adult class give impetus to such a ministry? The teacher may be nothing more than catalyst in such activity, or he may need to become the "project manager," seeing to all the details necessary to maintain the service.

Doubt and Encouragement

Mark 9 presents an intriguing picture of one caught "in the middle of faith," believing and yet doubting, doubting and yet believing. Many adults have daily interaction with those similarly caught. Some of their friends and associates could easily express the same "If you can" (Mark 9:22) to Jesus. How can the adult class step into the lives of such individuals and build their faith in the power of Jesus?

Testimony is a key to faith development. All through the Gospels men and women build faith in others by affirming what Jesus did for them. A simple card and note from a friend who has experienced the loss of a loved one and felt the comforting hand of God's Spirit may be just what a struggling believer needs at a time of personal loss. Sending an impersonal sympathy card—even if it carries a personal signature—will probably leave the same sense of isolation and loneliness it finds. But a personal "I-know-what-he-did-for-me" card brings both association and fellowship. The teacher may need to begin the practice of modeling such an approach in his own sympathy cards to class members, but the model set before a whole class has potential for a quicker, broader change.

Awe and Anticipation

In Mark 4:35-41, Jesus' power demonstrates itself in an altogether different realm: the order in the natural sciences. His ability to intervene in the laws of nature is always awe inspiring. Living in the twenty-first century has taken away some of the marvel from the marvelous. A class project to remind friends and families of God's power in nature could be faith enhancing

Discuss with your class "tag lines" that could be added to E-mails, faxes, telephone voice mail, and the like. Such tags can declare the glory of God in electronics science. For example, "Isn't God good? He created magnetism and allowed us to discover its values!" Or, "Created in God's image, we get to communicate with one another as he has communicated with us!" Or "It took ancient scribes months to copy long documents. We can do it with a 'Control/C.' Praise the Lord!"

A display board in the classroom, with a theme such as "By God's Design," can remind adult learners of the grand intricacy and inter-relatedness of his creation. A lesson on Mark 7:1-15 could be enhanced by a display on nutrition; a look of Matthew 9:20-22 would profit from a display on blood. Mark 7:31-37 is one of many texts that beg for an information board on hearing and deafness, while the account of Bartimaeus (Mark 10:46-52) lends itself to a display on sight and blindness. A teacher who has class members with training and/or personal experience in any of these subjects would bless the class member and the class by asking for that person's help.

For those who like big plans: an adult class could sponsor a children's science fair in the church with a theme such as "God Puts the Marvel in Marvelous," or " . . . the Awe in Awesome," or "God Is There in Little and Big" (emphasizing design in creation). A class-endowed cash prize and/or gifts of children's books on creation science may well encourage participation. Working with the church's children's leadership would have the happy benefit of establishing a sense of unity and fellowship often missing between adult classes and the children. And the resulting learner projects can offer a potential learning activity for any who visit the resultant displays. Most church facilities have a fellowship space that could be "adorned" with such projects for at least one weekend for interested worshipers.

Arts and Crafts

Many adults spend leisure time pursuing arts and crafts. The perceptive teacher will look for ways such interests can be applied to group studies. Whether in the visual arts, graphic arts, musical arts, or construction arts, interested group members could produce a variety of useful and aesthetic items in relationship to truths being studied.

In connection with a study of Mark 2, badge and button makers could produce something as simple as a pin with a stethoscope design to be given to class members as a reminder (and conversation starter) of Mark 2:17: "It is not the healthy who need a doctor, but the sick. I have not come to call the righteous, but sinners." A heart pin could be an effective reinforcement for a lesson based on Mark 7:1-23.

A musically talented learner could write a simple chorus on a key verse, such as Mark 5:36: "Don't be afraid; just believe." Teaching it to the class would add the double blessing, first to the composer, and then to the class.

A model-building enthusiast could provide a replica of a first-century fishing boat for illustration in a lesson on Matthew 13, Mark 4:35-41, or John 21:1-14.

A person who enjoys graphic design on the computer could prepare a number of items for group distribution in relation to Bible texts studied. A decorative and laminated bookmark with a key verse could encourage Bible memorization and use. A sheet with a border of human eyes could become a "Thank You, God" log of things a person sees for a week for which he or she is most thankful. This could be used for a follow-up on a lesson that includes the healing of a blind person. A skilled photographer could provide images of people being baptized for use in a lesson that includes the baptism of Jesus or of any of the many occasions in Acts that includes believers being baptized.

Going Around Doing Good

Give your learners something to do. Give them something good to do. You may be surprised at the learning that comes, at the growth that occurs.

HEADLINES AND HEADLINERS

A Creative Way to Summarize Biblical Truths

by Ronald G. Davis

Some Bible texts, especially from narrative historical sections, can lead to a "Big News" series of studies, focusing on politicians, pundits, prophets, and patrons. Death and destruction, failure and foolishness, fill the pages of Scripture. Had there been printing presses and journalists, the headlines would have been bold and blaring. Such were the times of the days of the Divided Kingdom of Israel and Judah.

When God's prophets tried to catch the attention of God's people with graphic and pithy words, the people ignored them. They could not—or chose not to—listen and heed. When God's spokesmen unfurled the banners of truth, the people of Israel and Judah used them to shine their idols and polish their accumulated gold. It turned out to be the way of death.

Capsules and Captions

Perceptive teachers and writers have long recognized the great learning value of capsulized truths—short, memorable statements that summarize the bigger, deeper truths of the lesson. Indeed, lesson titles themselves serve much the same function (and probably deserve much more attention and notice than most adult teachers give to them). Having such statements on regular display in the classroom offers real reinforcement and review possibilities. Having learners compose "headlines" based on the lesson texts offers opportunities for genuine reflection and reasoning.

The Teacher as "Editor"

In the field of journalism, editors often have the task of determining titles or section headings within a given piece of material. The Sunday school teacher of adults can play the same role in the classroom, giving titles to the parts or to the whole of a particular lesson.

As an introductory exercise to a series of lessons focusing on the Divided Kingdom, a "front page" of the *Jerusalem Journal* or the *Samaria Sunset* could carry an item to represent each lesson in the series. Compare the following "headlines" with the lesson texts to be studied. Can you match each one with a text? Try your skill; then check your responses with the answers below.

• "King Opts for Youth Movement in His Council"	1. 1 Kings 12:3-16
• "Relocation Plans in Full Swing"	2. 1 Kings 17:1-16
• "Meteorological Madman Menaces Monarch"	3. 1 Kings 18:20-39
• "New Song Sweeps Charts"	4. 1 Kings 22:15-28
• "Mountaintop Experience Proves Fatal"	5. Amos 1:1,2; 2:4-10
• "Bad News—Good News; Which Do You Want?"	6. Amos 4:2-5; 5:18-24
• "Prophet Lies to Tell the Truth"	7. Hosea 1:2–2:4
• "Local Man Called to Be Prophet"	8. Hosea 11:1-9
• "Three or Four Is Enough"	9. Micah 3:5-12; 6:3-8
• "Redevelopment of Urban Areas Planned"	10. Isaiah 6
• "Lions and Bears and Serpents—Oh, My!"	11. Isaiah 7
• "Once Loved, Twice Rejected"	12. Isaiah 5
• "Holy Man Marries Unholy Woman"	13. 2 Kings 17:6-18

Here is the suggested order of how the lessons are matched with the headlines: lessons 1, 13, 2, 12, 3, 11, 4, 10, 5, 9, 6, 8, 7. Did you decide differently on some? Good! From such differences of opinion and interpretation, a worthy discussion and explanation can often result. This is just the kind of careful thinking every teacher of adults wants to see in the class. (A teacher might want to display a large replica of a "front page" in the classroom and add relevant "headlines" week by week throughout the study.)

This same kind of headline display can be used with an individual lesson: create and display a headline for each verse, but do not identify the verse it represents. Then have the learners match each headline with the appropriate verse. Consider this example for Hosea 1:2–2:4: 1:2, "Finding a Wife In Israel"; 1:3, "Prophet Weds Suddenly"; 1:4, "Jezreel to Be Reeled In"; 1:5, "When the Bow Breaks"; 1:6, "Daughter Given Merciless Name"; 1:7, "Army Not Good Enough to Defend Judah"; 1:8, "Third Child Not a Charm"; 1:9, "Contract to Be Broken"; 1:10, "Population Projected to Reach Uncountable Numbers"; 1:11, "Two Nations to Be Reunited Under One King"; 2:1, "Stop Thinking in Negatives"; 2:2, "Leader Calls for New Morality"; 2:3, "Naked Ambition; Unquenchable Thirst"; 2:4, "Children Suffer From Parents' Mistakes"

Displaying or simply reading such headlines in random order and asking the class to match each to a relevant verse can encourage close examination of the text. Again, occasional disagreement can be used to good learning advantage.

Another idea is to reveal or read all "headlines" in the same order as the verses, asking learners to explain how each headline capsulizes (or fails to capsulize) the main idea of a specific verse. Class members may well be able to "edit" certain headlines to represent better the truth stated in each.

For example, suggesting that the word *Adulterous* be inserted before *Parents'* in the entry for Hosea 2:4 may be an improvement.

A third way the teacher can serve as "editor" is to give the class several "headlines" for a lesson (or a lesson segment or verse) and ask the group to decide which is the best one to represent the truth presented. Consider these three headline choices for 1 Kings 17: "Where's Elijah? Witnesses See Him One Place, Then Another"; "Prophet Curses King, Comforts Pagan Woman"; "From A (Ahab) to Z (Zarephath), Elijah Goes." Ask learners to choose which headline best summarizes the lesson truth and to be prepared to "defend" their choices

The Learner as "Reporter"

Although a teacher can encourage thinking through capsulized truths that he has written, even more thinking takes place when the learners must create the words. Before a teacher asks the learners to do some "headline writing," he will probably have to demonstrate the activity with one of the ideas suggested above. But once he does, some learners will find themselves doing the activity mentally as they look at different texts and lessons.

One simple way to get started is to work collectively, either as a class or in small groups. Asking for a list of "key words" is a good place to begin. For a lesson from 1 Kings 12, the list would probably include such words as *Rehoboam, yoke, lighter, advice, old, young, scorpions*, and others. Once the group has a list, call for someone to incorporate as many as possible in a summary statement. For the words suggested above, one might propose, "Rehoboam Rejects the Old, Takes Advice of the Young." Someone with a bit more imagination might suggest, "King Readies a Yoke of Scorpions: Watch Out!" One of the learners might develop the list of key words and ideas with the entire group and then ask smaller groups to pen the "headlines." These headlines can be shared with everyone after some deliberation

A second way to have learners devise the "headline" statements would be to give each learner a verse from the lesson text and to ask each to compose a headline for the verse's main idea. Several words in the verse should be highlighted, particularly verbs and other key words. Ask the learners to use one or more of the highlighted words or related words in each headline. One could highlight 2 Kings 17:6 for such an activity as follows: "In the ninth year of Hoshea, the *king* of Assyria *captured* Samaria and *deported* the Israelites to Assyria. He settled them in Halah, in Gozan on the Habor River and in the *towns* of the Medes." Verse 7 could be marked as, "All this took place because the Israelites had *sinned* against the Lord their God, who had brought them up out of Egypt from under the power of Pharaoh king of Egypt. They *worshiped* other *gods*." Imaginative class members will create headlines such as "Israel Removed by Ruler's Relocation Plan" (v. 6) and "Faithless Israelites Forget; Fear False Gods" (v. 7). Having each adult read the headline that he or she prepared and calling for others to identify the relevant verse will facilitate a careful look at the text and what it says.

Of course, if the class is in the habit of participating in a variety of writing activities, all the teacher will need to do is ask members to create "headlines" for units, lessons, or verses. And they can be encouraged by being reminded that there are no right and wrong answers. Headlines can be matter-of-fact, declarative statements, enigmatic phrases, or alliterative axioms. Though brief, they can plant the seed of a "germ idea" that will often result in a full-grown, fruitful plant. That's what every teacher of adults wants and that's what the Lord's kingdom must produce: mature, reproducing disciples.

The church needs a few more headlines touting the good news of good deeds done. The church needs a few more headliners, willing to step forward so that Jesus Christ can be lifted up before others who need to see the gospel in action. Making both the church and Christ more attractive to the world—that's exactly what Bible study is designed to accomplish. That's exactly what the teacher of adults wants to happen.

HERE'S A QUESTION . . .

Stimulating Discussion in the Classroom

by Brent L. Amato

Howard Hendricks said, "It's not what's taught, but what is caught." Such a statement begs the question, "How do I determine whether my students are connecting with me and learning from my teaching?" If I do nothing more than lecture in my class, it will be very difficult to evaluate how much my students are connecting. Something more is needed. Questions are part of the answer!

Before we dig into the what, which, and how of questions, keep in mind that there are two overarching questions that every lesson must answer. The first is So what? Nothing will be "caught" unless learners see relevance. The second question is Now what? This will help the students move toward an obedient response to the lesson. Without it, nothing might change!

What Is Communicated

What can questions communicate to your students about you? First of all, they show that your focus is on the students. Learners understand that you came to class with them on your mind. We teachers often get consumed by our teaching and our lessons—so much so that we may overlook our students! Your questions can communicate to your students that they're important, and they count for more than attendance. They show you're sincerely glad they came, and maybe even that they are appreciated.

Questions are an effective way to draw out the less vocal, energize the disinterested, direct the disruptive, and affirm all the students you teach. Questions are not so easily ignored as affirmations. When a teacher links several statements together in a running monologue, it's easy for a student to tune the teacher out. But a question snaps the student back to attention; a question demands an answer. Students will form answers in their minds even if they are not called on to speak their answers aloud.

Which Questions to Use and Not Use

Some questions are more effective than others. Less effective questions are closed (requiring only a yes/no or brief answer), overly complex, vague, "leading" (based on a hidden or not so hidden agenda of the teacher), confusing, or insignificant (detracting from the main idea of the lesson). Such questions may stifle the learning process.

Well-designed questions stimulate thought, with no "pat" answers. Better questions often are application-oriented; they force the learners to consider their own situations and see what the lesson text says about that. Such questions will be answered differently in a class of young adults, most of whom are single, from the way they will be answered in a class full of grandparents. Good questions take time to develop, so they should be prepared in advance.

How They Help

Questions were a large part of Jesus' teaching style. What can we learn from him? Jesus, the master teacher, used questions to determine desires (John 5:6), stimulate thinking (Luke 9:25), restore a relationship (John 21:15-17), challenge customs (Matthew 15:3), and encourage faith (Mark 4:40). Are you doing this in your classroom with the questions you use?

Jesus also used sequential questions to clarify attitudes and convictions. Consider these: "Who do people say the Son of Man is? . . . But what about you? . . . Who do you say I am?" (Matthew 16:13, 15). These simple yet profound questions helped the disciples move beyond public opinion to personal confession.

Further Questions

But I'm sure you still have questions about questions. How do "declarations of truth" fit with questions? You need both. How long should you wait in silence for an answer to your question? For adults, 60 seconds (maintaining eye contact and restating the question, if necessary) is not too long. If there is no answer to your question, should you answer it? Try not to. Can you answer a question with a question? Why not? Should you always allow time for questions? Yes.

If there are no further questions, start preparing to ask some good ones. Then watch what happens to your relationships with your students, to class interaction, and to "what is caught"!

His Stories—and Ours

Using Stories to Teach the Story of Jesus

by Ronald G. Davis

As soon as the two disciples of Jesus realized what had happened to them on the road to Emmaus, they had to find those who would want to know "what had happened on the way" (Luke 24:35). History is simply the things done "on the way" to doing daily life. Every person is a part of history. Every person has a history.

Luke wanted to tell the story of Jesus, even as it was "handed down to us by those who from the first were eyewitnesses and servants of the word" (Luke 1:2). Luke wanted to tell the stories of Jesus—the most important personal history ever lived. And his Gospel reflects his high esteem for stories, or narratives, as the way to communicate the truth of history.

Any quick skimming of Luke's Gospel in a Bible version that uses paragraph headings is a journey through an index of one narrative after another. Luke's Gospel has more "stories"—that is, distinct narrative segments—than any other Gospel. In fact, about three-fourths of Luke's Gospel is narrative. And much of the material that is not narrative appears in the context of a narrative, such as when Jesus discussed future events on the occasion of walking by the temple area with his disciples (Luke 21:5-36). From Luke 9:51 through 18:14 Luke relates twenty-one stories that the other Gospels do not include.

Such a concern with narrative helped Luke achieve his purpose for writing his Gospel: to establish "the certainty of the things [Theophilus had] been taught" (Luke 1:4). This concern for truth is seen in the Old Testament as well—from the events in Eden to the conflicts of Ezra and Nehemiah's time. History reveals who God is and what his will is. History is truly "his story."

Stories and Wise Teachers

Let us consider how much teachers of adults can learn from others who have attempted to communicate the truth of God's Word in story form.

While reading stories to adults may seem childish or out of place, this is a teaching method that can foster a wide range of learning opportunities for adults. Few learners of any age can resist listening to a good, well-told story. Reading aloud to adult students probably should seldom exceed 400 to 500 words, and it should not last any longer than four to five minutes. While our major source of stories for reading (or telling) is the Bible itself, we must not overlook the wealth of significant stories to be gleaned from non-biblical sources.

"Read Me a Bible Story, Teacher"

All the stories of the Bible have been told and retold in print. Some of these endeavors have followed biblical texts closely, while others have used a well-informed imagination. (And some, of course, have used uninformed imaginations!) The "bare bones" nature of the biblical accounts is by the Holy Spirit's design, so that (as John observed) we do not have to deal with an unmanageable collection of books (John 21:25).

Even stories published for children can provide ready instructional material for adults. Excellent compare-and-contrast activities and discussions can ensue. However, one must be cautious of any retellings that ignore or deny the inspirational, revelational nature of the contents of the Bible. At the same time, such retellings may offer useful insights into the thinking of those who consider biblical stories to be in the same category as myth and legend (and they will offer your students a strong reminder that there are those who hold such views and who seek to influence children through their writings).

Studies from Luke's Gospel include some of the most familiar portions of Jesus' life and ministry: the beautiful birth narratives, the parable of the prodigal son, Zaccheus's unique encounter with Christ, and the dramatic events surrounding Jesus' death and his resurrection from the dead. As was the case in Luke's day, many have "taken in hand," as Luke himself did (Luke 1:1), the pen of narration and applied it to these and other stories.

Every religious publisher that prepares materials for children will have a selection of usable titles. (Most churches have such books in their children's classrooms.) And most public libraries, in the religious section for children, shelve many relevant titles. Although the diligent searcher will find other good choices, a few worthy titles from Luke follow.

Award-winning Christian writer Madeleine L'Engle prepared a series of stories on the life of Christ in *The Glorious Impossible* (Simon and Schuster, Inc., New York, 1990). This includes a telling of "The Annunciation."

The beautifully and authentically illustrated *The Blessing of the Lord* by Gary D. Schmidt (William B. Eerdmans Publishing Company, Grand Rapids, 1997), with artwork by Dennis Nolan, includes stories on "The Centurion at Calvary" and "Anna, Simeon, and the Blessing Fulfilled." Though these retellings are long, a teacher could use only selected portions for reading to the class.

One very popular series for children has been the Arch book collection from Concordia Publishing House. These versified retellings range from fair to excellent, but can be read quickly and with easy articulation and emphasis. Stories from the life and the parables of Jesus offer ready possibilities for use during a series from Luke's Gospel. (And adults might also enjoy the illustrations, which are easy to show as the text is being read!)

Holiday House, Inc., a leading New York publisher for children, has published a variety of religious titles, such as, *He Is Risen: The Easter Story* by Elizabeth Winthrop (1985), with illustrations by the noted children's artist Charles Mikolaycak. And popular children's writer/illustrator Tomie dePaola has done some significant work for Holiday House, including *The Miracles of Jesus* and *The Parables of Jesus.*

It is always interesting to compare and contrast what human writers do with a biblical account with what the inspired writer has recorded. Sadly, several items are omitted even while non-biblical events are added. Even worse, some factual information is distorted and denied. Most adults, however, will gain much from discussing the differences and the possible reasons for them. When a writer violates cultural, historical, or geographical facts, one is right to question his motives—or at least his understanding. This, of course, demands that the teacher and the members of the class have a solid background in the cultural, historical, and geographical setting of the biblical narratives.

"Read Me More Stories, Teacher"

Many other stories worthy of use in instructing adults can be drawn from non-biblical sources, both from the realms of fiction and non-fiction (especially biography). Tales from literature may help one illustrate the importance of standards of right and wrong, or, conversely, may highlight the contrasting worldview based on humanistic thinking. Even the well-known fables of Aesop can illustrate both, for not only is diligent effort touted as the secret to personal success (as in "The Ant and the Grasshopper"), but the "get-even" mentality is represented in "The Fox and the Stork," with the usual concluding moral stated: "One bad turn deserves another." (That's quite the opposite of the behavior taught by Jesus in the "Golden Rule.") And other fables from anonymous sources, such as "The Goose That Laid the Golden Egg," illustrate quite effectively the consequences of greed, which is one of the key issues of Jesus' parable of the dishonest manager in Luke 12.

Of course, there is a wealth of biographical material that is worthy of use by the teacher, especially incidents from the lives of the "saints." These include vivid accounts from the classic *Foxe's Book of Martyrs* (originally compiled by John Foxe) to more contemporary examples of godly lives, such as those of Corrie Ten Boom and Aleksandr Solzhenitsyn. The hesitation of potential disciples in Luke 9:57-62 can certainly be brought to life using some of the incidents recorded in Foxe's collection or some of Solzhenitsyn's stories of life in a Siberian gulag.

Finally, the teacher of adults must not overlook the compelling stories that appear in the daily news. These accounts show how man's behavior has changed little from the first century to the twenty-first. Prodigal son (and prodigal daughter) stories abound, for sin still abounds. Reading such items to the class (keep them fairly short) and asking for the way(s) in which a story parallels biblical incidents will elicit both thought and insight—and this is exactly what the teacher of adults is after.

The Teacher's "Library"

Every wise teacher of adults should constantly be "collecting" stories that may prove to be useful in instruction. Keeping an eye on coming lessons and coming lesson series will enable one to spot just the right stories. Those read to children and grandchildren, those found in devotional and leisure reading, those heard or seen in daily news reports—all have the potential to become effective instructional material.

Who can resist a good story? Almost no one. Jesus knew that, and so did his Father. What about you?

Imitating Jesus' Inclusive Ministry

Including Persons With Disabilities in Your Teaching

by Jim Pierson

Jeff Jackson (not his real name) is included in his Sunday school class at First Church. That may sound unremarkable unless you understand that Jeff has mental retardation and physical disabilities. That, however, has not prevented him from being accepted by the members of his class. They take turns caring for him. They call him each day, drive him to church activities, and take him to his doctor's appointments. They share in his life in many significant ways.

Today there are some 54 million Jeffs living in the United States. In fact, in every community one will find people who have mental, sensory, physical, emotional, and communication disabilities, which may prevent their participation in many life functions. These people need to be included in the Sunday school, in the church, and in the lives of church members. Such inclusion mirrors Jesus' inclusive approach.

Jesus regularly encountered people with disabilities. Matthew 9 describes a series of such encounters. He healed a man with a physical disability (v. 2). He cured a woman of a disease she had endured for 12 years (v. 20). He restored the sight of two men (vv. 29, 30); then he met and rehabilitated a man with a speech problem (vv. 32, 33). Whatever the disability, Jesus made a difference.

Your adult class can also make a difference in the lives of students with disabilities. Consider the following suggestions, and imitate Jesus' inclusive approach in your own particular setting.

Sensory and Physical Disabilities

If a student's disability is deafness, find a volunteer interpreter to communicate the lesson. Ask the interpreter to conduct some sign language classes for the class members. Learning a few basic signs will make the student feel more a part of the group. If the student is not completely without hearing, other means of help are in order. If the person lip-reads, she must have a clear view of the teacher's face. Instruct class members not to talk louder or shout to her, for doing so can interfere with her normal processes of communication.

If the disability is blindness, invite the person to the class. Orient him to the classroom and the path he will need to take to get there. Ask class members not to move furniture or other objects without telling the blind person. Provide a Braille Bible and other materials. Address the person by name. Tell class members that it is important to let the person know who they are (also, remember that blind people may find it difficult to recall names, since they cannot match a face with a name). Give explanations of items being written on the chalkboard. If the person uses a guide dog, explain why other members of the class should not pet the dog. Be sure to offer transportation to the person as necessary.

It is also helpful to know some basic skills for guiding a person who is blind. For example, the folded arm provides the basic point of reference for the person. Moving the elbow back suggests that the person is to sit behind you. Stopping indicates that you are nearing a step or a curb.

The teacher may have special concerns about copying materials for a student who is not completely blind, but is visually impaired. You do not need special permission to enlarge the pages of one book for such a student. Whenever you need more than one copy of a page, contact the publisher for permission.

If the disability involves other physical limitations, make the building and the classroom area accessible. When social activities are planned, try to take care of accessibility barriers ahead of time. Familiarize yourself with any special equipment such as wheelchairs and/or braces.

Often some of the physical problems that classes of older adults must address are those experienced by people who have had strokes. If someone who has had a stroke has been an active part of the class, keep her involved. Offer to provide transportation or assistance with activities that may now be difficult for the person to handle independently. Even if communication is difficult, continue to try. Look the person in the eye. Make statements instead of asking questions. Visit the person at home. Let her know she is still an important part of the group.

A friend of mine used to play golf every Thursday with three other men from his Sunday school class. Then he had a stroke, and his former golfing buddies at first didn't know what to do. But with a little creativity, the problem was solved. A new fourth person was added to the group, and my friend continues to be a part of the group—only now he enjoys the action, along with the fresh air and sunshine, from his golf cart. He is still in Sunday school as well.

Other Types of Disabilities

If an individual's problem is emotional, be understanding and supportive—both of him and his family. Ask the family or the person about the nature of the problem, the treatment, and what the class can do to help. You may want to ask a mental health professional to come to a class function and discuss the nature of mental illness.

If the problem is a learning disability, be cautious and be sensitive to the person's needs. Never ask a visitor or new member to read aloud in class without checking with him or her ahead of time. Often poor reading is a noticeable symptom of a learning disability.

If the disability involves communication (and this is common), develop a successful means of communicating with the person. Never pretend that you understand. Ask the person to repeat a statement or say it in a different way. A home visit may lead to workable communication solutions involving both the classroom and class members. It might not hurt to have pencil and paper handy; if the person is able to read, she can indicate by nodding or by other signals whether or not her message is being understood.

If the disability is mental retardation, the process of inclusion will require more attention. If this involves only one or two people, include them in the regular class. Encourage class members to take turns sitting with them, assisting them with finding Scripture references, making interactions with other class members easier, looking out for them at class parties, and getting to know what nice people they really are.

Additional Avenues of Service

If more than two individuals with mental retardation are attending your church, the church should consider organizing a special class just for them. This class would have its own teacher and lesson, but the opening prayer time, refreshments, and social activities could be a joint endeavor. Such an arrangement provides an opportunity for mutual ministry and fellowship, while offering a program of Bible study and learning activities geared specifically to your special adults.

Class members can also volunteer with organizations that help persons with disabilities. A call to the appropriate organizations in your city or town will reveal a variety of needs.

Finally, the adult class can minister by being sensitive to the needs of a family dealing with a disability. If such a family is part of your class, take time to learn their needs. If this disability involves a child in the family, keep in mind the four occasions when this family may require special attention: (1) when they learn the diagnosis, (2) when the child starts to school, (3) when the child leaves the school system (because the parents will no longer have access to the services provided by the school), and (4) when the parents realize that they can no longer provide care for their child. Often the most critical service parents need is respite care. In its simplest form, this means having an extra pair of hands to help with specific tasks. Parents will also appreciate the kindness of someone who will offer to watch their child so that they can go out for special occasions.

Be There!

Perhaps the best advice is just "Be there!" One Sunday our minister announced that Mrs. Johnson's daughter would be moving to a residential facility. On moving day, a member of Mrs. Johnson's Sunday school class arrived at her house and spent the day. She said, "If my daughter were moving away from home, I would want someone to be with me. That is the reason I am here." After helping to arrange the furniture in the daughter's new residence, she drove Mrs. Johnson back to her apartment. Later that day, another member of the class took Mrs. Johnson out for dinner.

People such as Mrs. Johnson and Jeff Jackson represent unique opportunities for your adult Sunday school class to mirror Jesus' compassion and his ministry of inclusion. By doing so, your class members will receive much more than they give; and they will be ministered to in ways they never imagined.

IT'S THEIR STORY TOO!

Making Genesis Come Alive

by Eleanor A. Daniel

I love stories! Most people do. Stories excite the imagination and stimulate thinking. Your challenge is to use stories in such a way that your learners travel with you on a progressive journey to see God at work.

A series of lessons from Genesis provides a great opportunity for story-telling. Genesis involves great narratives that demonstrate an unfolding drama of God in relation to his creation and his people. These narratives invite us to adopt them as a part of our own faith story. Your success as a teacher in this regard will help prevent your learners from approaching the studies as a mere series of facts.

You will do more than tell stories, of course. But don't ignore the fact that adults respond well to them. Part of your task is to ask questions that engage learners in their own involvement in the story line. Consider the following story development ideas and questions.

Genesis 1:1-25. Don't get bogged down in theoretical discussions of cosmology that cannot be adequately addressed during your brief class. Instead, begin where the text does: "In the beginning God." *Questions*: Reflecting on the creation account in Genesis, what does it tell you about God and yourself for humans to have been created in his image? Adding Psalm 8 to your reflection, what response is appropriate to our Creator God?

Genesis 1:26-31. Pick up the story from the earlier part of Genesis 1 and expand on the nature of humankind as created in God's image. Emphasize God's intention to create those who could interact with him. *Question*: Though marred by sin, what glimpses do we see of people expressing the image of God?

Genesis 12 and 15. Connect these two narratives to paint the agony of waiting for a promise that no longer seemed to be fulfillable. *Question*: In what ways did Abraham's responses make him a model—or perhaps not a model at all—for you as you wait on God in your life?

Genesis 21. Return to the story of God's promise that Abraham would have a son, and show how Abraham tried to resolve his wait for a son. Then cast the story to show the consequences

result from trying to solve problems on our own terms. *Questions*: How was Abraham shaped by the choices he made? How are you shaped by the choices you make?

Genesis 24. Check out marriage customs of the patriarchs! Emphasize the importance of finding a spouse in the larger clan to allow for a continuity that would please God. Stress that marriage is a sacred, spiritual contract. The choice we make has profound implications for our relationship with God. *Questions*: How do you see these facts demonstrated in this story? How do you see them demonstrated in the lives of those you know?

Genesis 25. Emphasize how differences among siblings can create rivalry, especially when parents express disappointment or delight with one child or make overt comparisons between children. *Questions*: How can sibling rivalries affect a person's future? How have you seen this develop?

Genesis 28. Emphasize how Jacob was invited into the same covenant as Abraham. *Questions*: Why was it important for God to confirm to Jacob his place in the covenant? Why is an understanding of *covenant with God* important for every believer?

Genesis 29. Shape the story to emphasize Jacob's deep love for Rachel. *Question*: What does Jacob teach us (positively or negatively) about response to disappointment?

Genesis 33. Focus on reconciliation and how to achieve it. *Question*: What does this account teach us about reconciliation?

Genesis 37. Examine how rivalry can result in mistreatment. *Question*: If you had been 17-year-old Joseph, what would have been your thoughts as you were sold into Egypt?

Genesis 41. Continue to emphasize Joseph's profound disappointments and God's continuing affirmation of him. *Question*: What difference do you think it made to Joseph's character to endure the difficulties he experienced?

Genesis 45. Emphasize Joseph's part in protecting God's people. *Question*: How was Joseph able to maintain a perspective about God's work in his life?

Genesis 48. Provide an overview of the waning days of Jacob's (Israel's) life. *Questions*: What legacy did Jacob consider to be most important to his sons? What do you think is important for your own family in this regard?

Enjoy the great narratives of God's work that are set forth in Genesis. More importantly, make them your own (and your learners') narratives as well!

LEADING THE DISCUSSION
Setting and Tips

by James Riley Estep, Jr.

"Don't teachers just use discussion as a time-filler? I mean, some teachers come unprepared, then fill the class time with discussion!"

Unfortunately, we all have experienced discussions that fizzled. As with any teaching method, discussion sometimes is used *unintentionally*, meaning without a purpose and design. Discussions that lack purpose and design can indeed degenerate into pointless time-filling. The result may be a meandering exercise in the sharing of personal experience and perspective. When discussion is not directed toward a learning goal, you may hear one of your small groups discussing who's playing in the football game later that afternoon rather than discussing, say, the significance of Ruth in the lineage of King David. This is called *discussion drift*. How do we fix this problem?

When properly used, discussion can be a most effective teaching method that values the input from your learners. Discussion sends the signal that the teacher's viewpoint is not the only valid one in the class, but that the insights, perspectives, and experiences of the students are also important. Discussion also can teach participants how to think biblically about life decisions and circumstances in a classroom environment before facing the issues in real life.

Setting the Stage

Using discussion as an effective method of teaching requires that you set the stage in four ways. *First, make sure to use purposeful, open-ended questions.* Discussion often fizzles as a teaching method because the question the teacher poses is not capable of fostering discussion. Questions that require a simple factual answer or that can be answered *yes* or *no* fall into this category.

For example, one teacher might ask, "Does the Bible describe Ruth as an ancestor of King David?" Answer: "Well, yes." How can anyone *discuss* such a question? While any given discussion question can have a desired outcome—something on which the rest of the lesson can build—the question should not be so "closed" that it does not allow an open exchange of ideas.

Now think of this question: "Why is Ruth's ancestry in King David's lineage significant?" This kind of question calls for more than a one-word response. Such a question calls for the student to analyze and synthesize biblical material. They have to *think*, not simply recall.

Second, you as a teacher have to be mentally prepared to use discussion. Your mental preparation as teacher includes the realization that your role is somewhat different from what it is in the lecture. You as teacher must see yourself not as the sage-on-the-stage, but as a guide-at-the-side.

Many times teachers think their role is to respond quickly to questions with the "correct" answer. But when using discussion, the teacher often will turn questions back to the class to keep the discussion going. There will be time for the teacher to provide his or her own thoughts once the class has had an opportunity to wrestle with the question. Learners will be more receptive to the teacher's thoughts once they have had a chance to discuss the matter. This requires a certain amount of patience as you assist students in working through difficult questions for themselves.

Teachers using the discussion method also must know how to respond gently to a student whose response is way off base. Promoting discussion doesn't mean that you will allow heretical suggestions to go unchallenged. Even so, a certain amount of gentleness is needed here. Too firm of a response to a student may cause others in the class to become hesitant in sharing their ideas for fear of a negative response from the teacher.

Your mental preparation also should include being thoroughly familiar with the lesson material. Such preparation often will need to be more extensive than it would be when using lecture. In a lecture format, the teacher knows exactly what is to be said and how it is to be said. Under a discussion format, the teacher's preparation includes anticipating the possible responses of students in order to be able to address them. Of course, you can't be prepared for every possible question. In that case, don't pretend! Be honest and say, "I don't really know, but I will look into it."

Third, prepare your students in advance for discussion. Discussion will fizzle if students are not ready for it. Suppose you announce, "Today we are going to discuss Ruth," but students were not asked to read Ruth prior to class or e-mailed a list of possible discussion questions to investigate. As a result, students enter class cognitively cold but are expected to heat up very quickly!

Effective discussions are those in which the students are equipped to engage. If students are neither informed about the subject nor provided relevant information, then their discussion is more likely to end up being a pooling of ignorance, a grasping for truth in the dark, or an occasion to talk about the big football game. The result is a discussion that does not achieve your learning goals.

This problem is avoided by providing students with relevant material in advance. This material can take the form of print media (for example, a quarterly curriculum student book) or digital media (for example, a web site that includes information about upcoming lessons). Students also can be provided with a list of possible discussion questions in advance (perhaps by e-mail) so they can think about appropriate responses. Informed students make for an informed discussion and a genuine learning environment.

Fourth, a learning environment conducive to discussion will be a great help. The physical aspects of your learning space are important. In general, someone who walks into your learning space can make an educated guess as to what method of teaching is favored by the instructor (or, at least, which method of teaching the room is designed to support) just by looking at the layout. Classrooms that feature a front-and-center podium, a projector, and rows of seats facing forward scream "lecture!"

On the other hand, a classroom environment that favors discussion may have chairs in circles around tables. While such a classroom may have a podium, it will probably not be centered in front of the class, but located off to the side (being used to hold the teacher's notes). An environment conducive to discussion can also have a markerboard on which to write student ideas and responses.

When someone sees this kind of classroom, discussion is immediately assumed. After all, it is difficult to lecture to a class of students sitting at six round tables with some backs turned to you! When the environment is right, discussion is more readily used as a means of instruction.

Classroom Tips

Now that you know how to set the stage for discussion, we move to some practical tips. *First, make sure to provide the questions in written form.* This means writing them on the board, putting them on PowerPoint slides, or reproducing them on handouts. (If some students have their backs to the board or screen because they are sitting at round tables, handouts may be best.) Students should not have to ask, "Now, what question are we supposed to be discussing?" or "Can you say that again?"

Second, make sure to walk around the room if you are using a small-group discussion format. Don't just stay at the front of the class or walk into the hallway. Rather, roam throughout the class, listening to the group discussions. This allows you to know what might be brought up when the groups share their conclusions. It can also allow you to correct an erroneous idea while it is still contained within one discussion group.

Third, set a time limit for discussion. When the question is provided to the class, say, for example, "Take eight minutes to discuss this question." This helps you keep the class time flowing. It also keeps the groups on task, since they know they don't have time to meander.

Fourth, don't reveal all your questions at once. Occasionally, one discussion question will build on another. For example, consider these two questions from a lesson on Ruth: "How significant can one 'common person' be in the history of a nation?" and "How significant was Ruth's impact on biblical history?" Students may wrestle with the first question and conclude that common people have little significance in the grand sweep of history. But the second question will challenge that conclusion and force the participants to reconsider. The impact of the discussion may be diminished if you put both questions on the board at the same time.

Fifth, always bring closure. Using the discussion method does not mean allowing students to leave class with nothing more than questions. Provide directions, summations, and answers to the questions by utilizing their insights and the material you have prepared.

Finally, don't give up. The way to use discussion productively is to practice using it. Learn from the experience, correct your mistakes, and keep trying. It will be worth it!

"LET US REASON TOGETHER"

Using Study Groups in Teaching

by James Riley Estep, Jr.

Christian educators often advocate the use of small groups as a teaching method for adults. However, the effectiveness of this method sometimes falls short. This occurs when small group discussions become mere time-fillers or serve as little more than opportunities for fellowship over coffee. To maximize the learning potential of small groups, make them *study groups*.

What and Why?

In study groups, learners are asked to do more than merely reflect on personal experience or share perspective. Rather, a study group processes *content*. While group members may on occasion share in a personal way, that will be primarily a means of introducing the subject of the content to be learned. This maximizes the learning potential of the study group.

In the lecture method, the instructor "stands and delivers." It is a static method of teaching, since the teacher often does not plan for engagement or dialogue. The use of study groups is more dynamic. Not only does such a method *require* dialogue between the teacher and the learners, the learners themselves also will be engaged in dialogue among themselves. Thus the class is not only taught by the teacher, but also forms what may be thought of as minicommunities of learning that are centered on studying the biblical text. Thus everyone is involved in learning God's truth actively.

Teacher's Role

The use of study groups requires you as the teacher to prepare in four ways. First, you must *be prepared both to talk and to be silent!* You may have a ready answer to a question posed to the class (or posed by someone in the class), but you will need to harness your enthusiasm to share that answer until your learners have had adequate opportunity to discuss it among themselves. If your students perceive that you are going to give the "correct" answer to the question—no matter what anyone says in the discussion—they will hesitant to open up and share their thinking. Don't stifle the discussion by always giving the right answer.

Second, *you will need more intellectual preparation* for study groups than for the lecture method because of the near certainty that the groups will answer your questions differently from the way you would. Some of these answers are acceptable alternatives, but some will be wrong. You will find it helpful to think through in advance possible responses to the questions you will give your study groups. Be careful to note when someone's wording of a statement really expresses the correct answer in different terms from the way you would express it.

Third, you will have to *begin your lesson preparation earlier* in the week. The study group method can require handouts, at least, and possibly overhead transparencies or PowerPoint slides, objects, or games. You will need to have your lesson plan fully developed early enough in the week to allow time to create or secure these things.

Fourth, a vital part of your preparation will be to *arrive early in your classroom* since you may need to make physical changes in the seating arrangements to fit the study group method. Also, with more teaching materials to use, more time may be needed to set things up (example: getting your computer ready for a PowerPoint presentation). Preparation for the use of study groups often requires more work than other methods.

Making It Work

Five practices make for the effective use of study groups. First, allow students adequate time to share with one another. Let them know how many minutes they have to discuss an item; then give a one-minute warning that "time is almost up." Second, make an intentional decision when you form groups whether or not you want to keep couples together. Groups of odd numbers (three, five, etc.) allow for "unattached" students to feel like they fit in. Groups larger than eight usually don't work well.

Third, roam around while your students are in their groups. This lets you hear what directions the discussions are taking and redirect if needed. Fourth, write student responses on the board when that time comes. This conveys the fact that you value their responses. It also ensures that you are hearing them accurately. It also allows students to remember what has been said.

Fifth, try to affirm every answer. Rarely will a response be so off track that it deserves an outright No! Instead, affirm what is right in the answer, and then provide the correction. "I see your point, but . . ." or "Well, that would be true if . . ." will encourage discussion and dialogue without the fear of being slapped down for a "wrong" response.

No Fear!

Teachers of adults may avoid using small groups out of fear—fear of losing focus, fear of allowing personal interests to take over, fear that the Bible study will degenerate into a "what it means to me" outcome. But designing your small groups to be study groups will help your students benefit from a focused investigation of the content and proper application of Scripture. Try it!

Second, *you will need more intellectual preparation* for study groups than for the lecture method because of the near certainty that the groups will answer your questions differently from the way you would. Some of these answers are acceptable alternatives, but some will be wrong. You will find it helpful to think through in advance possible responses to the questions you will give your study groups. Be careful to note when someone's wording of a statement really expresses the correct answer in different terms from the way you would express it.

Third, you will have to *begin your lesson preparation earlier* in the week. The study group method can require handouts, at least, and possibly overhead transparencies or PowerPoint slides, objects, or games. You will need to have your lesson plan fully developed early enough in the week to allow time to create or secure these things.

Fourth, a vital part of your preparation will be to *arrive early in your classroom* since you may need to make physical changes in the seating arrangements to fit the study group method. Also, with more teaching materials to use, more time may be needed to set things up (example: getting your computer ready for a PowerPoint presentation). Preparation for the use of study groups often requires more work than other methods.

Making It Work

Five practices make for the effective use of study groups. First, allow students adequate time to share with one another. Let them know how many minutes they have to discuss an item; then give a one-minute warning that "time is almost up." Second, make an intentional decision when you form groups whether or not you want to keep couples together. Groups of odd numbers (three, five, etc.) allow for "unattached" students to feel like they fit in. Groups larger than eight usually don't work well.

Third, roam around while your students are in their groups. This lets you hear what directions the discussions are taking and redirect if needed. Fourth, write student responses on the board when that time comes. This conveys the fact that you value their responses. It also ensures that you are hearing them accurately. It also allows students to remember what has been said.

Fifth, try to affirm every answer. Rarely will a response be so off track that it deserves an outright No! Instead, affirm what is right in the answer, and then provide the correction. "I see your point, but . . ." or "Well, that would be true if . . ." will encourage discussion and dialogue without the fear of being slapped down for a "wrong" response.

No Fear!

Teachers of adults may avoid using small groups out of fear—fear of losing focus, fear of allowing personal interests to take over, fear that the Bible study will degenerate into a "what it means to me" outcome. But designing your small groups to be study groups will help your students benefit from a focused investigation of the content and proper application of Scripture. Try it!

"LET US REASON TOGETHER"

Using Study Groups in Teaching

by James Riley Estep, Jr.

Christian educators often advocate the use of small groups as a teaching method for adults. However, the effectiveness of this method sometimes falls short. This occurs when small group discussions become mere time-fillers or serve as little more than opportunities for fellowship over coffee. To maximize the learning potential of small groups, make them *study groups*.

What and Why?

In study groups, learners are asked to do more than merely reflect on personal experience or share perspective. Rather, a study group processes *content*. While group members may on occasion share in a personal way, that will be primarily a means of introducing the subject of the content to be learned. This maximizes the learning potential of the study group.

In the lecture method, the instructor "stands and delivers." It is a static method of teaching, since the teacher often does not plan for engagement or dialogue. The use of study groups is more dynamic. Not only does such a method *require* dialogue between the teacher and the learners, the learners themselves also will be engaged in dialogue among themselves. Thus the class is not only taught by the teacher, but also forms what may be thought of as minicommunities of learning that are centered on studying the biblical text. Thus everyone is involved in learning God's truth actively.

Teacher's Role

The use of study groups requires you as the teacher to prepare in four ways. First, you must *be prepared both to talk and to be silent!* You may have a ready answer to a question posed to the class (or posed by someone in the class), but you will need to harness your enthusiasm to share that answer until your learners have had adequate opportunity to discuss it among themselves. If your students perceive that you are going to give the "correct" answer to the question—no matter what anyone says in the discussion—they will hesitant to open up and share their thinking. Don't stifle the discussion by always giving the right answer.

Lots of Questions
Mastering the Master's Art

by Ronald G. Davis

Jesus was a Master of questions. Some of his questions were designed to elicit statements of faith. Some were designed to force thinking. Others were intended to put the one questioned on the spot. And though he could know the answer by divine insight, Jesus asked questions to "check on" the accomplished level of understanding in his learners.

Jesus asked Nathanael, "Because I said that I saw you under the fig tree, do you believe?" (paraphrased from John 1:50). Nicodemus was humbled by the query: "Are you a teacher in Israel and don't know basic spiritual truths?" (John 3:10). To the Jews who challenged his authority for healing on the Sabbath, Jesus simply questioned and observed: "If you don't really believe Moses' words, how can you believe mine?" (John 5:47). And to Philip—as the multitude approached in the wilderness of Galilee—he posed a stumper: "Where shall we buy bread for these thousands to eat?" (John 6:5). Poignantly he would have to ask the Twelve, "Will you go away just like the multitude of disciples?" (John 6:67). And his purpose was always to elicit the highest level of learner activity possible: thinking!

Questions may seem to have only a review and reinforcement purpose. On a much deeper level they force learners to compare, contrast, evaluate, analyze, synthesize, and apply. The perceptive teacher—in imitation of the Master—will ask questions and stir learner questions of all levels.

Tests as Questioning Activity

Though some Christian teachers resist the idea of testing, Jesus gave his learners tests. That is exactly what he was doing with Nicodemus when he arrived with commendation (John 3:1, 2) and with Philip by the Sea of Galilee as the crowd arrived with anticipation (John 6:1-6). (Both failed the tests!) A wholesale rejection of all testing shows a misunderstanding of the concept of instruction. Testing is a part of the teaching-learning phenomenon.

The classroom teacher can use tests for all the right reasons: to discover or verify learners' levels of understanding, to make the learners curious as to answers they do not have and to initiate their exploratory behavior toward finding answers, to review and reinforce facts and conclusions already studied, and to evaluate the learners' understanding after instruction.

All the traditional testing devices can be used: true-false statements, matching series, multiple-choice, fill-in-the-blank, and open-ended questions. Consider this emphasis on Hebrews 1:1-3 as the keynote verses for the writer's whole epistle: in the upper third of a sheet to be copied and given to each learner, print these verses with key words omitted; for example,

"In the _____ God spoke to our ancestors through the _____ at many times and in _____ ways, but in these _____ days he has spoken to us by his _____, whom he appointed _____ of all things, and through whom also he made the _____. The Son is the _____ of God's _____ and the exact _____ of his being, sustaining all things by his powerful _____. After he had provided _____ for _____, he sat down at the _____ hand of the _____ in heaven."

On the lower third of the sheet print the verses without omissions. Fold the bottom third up over the middle and tape the flap to keep it from easily falling open. As students arrive, hand them copies of the sheet and direct them to fill in the blanks as best they can—without using Bibles. As class begins (and as they are finished with the fill-in), direct them to untape the lower flaps and check their own tests. This will give you an effective focus toward introducing a key truth of the book of Hebrews: Jesus is God's final revelation, and he is superior in every way to God's earlier revelations of himself.

A simple multiple-choice series could offer a useful introduction to a Bible book about to be studied. Again, the epistle to the Hebrews could be introduced with questions such as the following (with answers in bold):

(1) As we have it divided, the book of Hebrews has ___ chapters. (A) 7, (B) 9, (C) 11, **(D) 13,** (E) 15

(2) One Old Testament person not given significant attention in Hebrews is (A) Aaron, (B) Abraham, (C) David, **(D) Joseph**, (E) Moses.

(3) Which of the following best characterizes the epistle to the Hebrews? (A) a summary of Old Testament history, with a messianic emphasis; (B) an extended appeal to Gentile Christians not to revert to paganism; **(C) a careful presentation of the superiority of Christ and the church over the Mosaic system;** (D) a collection of proverbs and wise sayings; (E) a refutation of arguments presented by first-century Judaizers.

(4) Melchizedek is the name of (A) an opponent of early Christianity in Rome, **(B) a high priest of God introduced in Genesis**, (C) the angel who revealed the message of this book to its writer, (D) the only person who is greeted at the end of the book, other than Timothy; (E) an unidentified book to which this epistle refers several times.

(5) Which of the following grand truths is from the epistle to the Hebrews? (A) "Contend for the faith," (B) "From infancy you have known the Holy Scriptures," (C) "Godliness with contentment is great gain," **(D) "How shall we escape, if we ignore so great a salvation?"** (E) "Our citizenship is in heaven."

(6) Which of the following places is named in the epistle? (A) Assyria, (B) Corinth, **(C) Egypt**, (D) Galatia, (E) Rome.

(7) In chapter 11, which of the following women is named? (A) Deborah, (B) Eve, (C) Miriam, (D) Rachel, **(E) Rahab**.

An occasional test will add variety to the classroom and will allow the teacher to accomplish various goals that are difficult to attain in any other activity.

Oral Interrogatives

Asking questions aloud to learners is not as simple as it seems. Whole books have been written as pedagogical studies on the "simple" use of questions in the classroom. Teachers tend to make three recurring mistakes: (1) they ask only factual questions that elicit little thought (these are matters of either-or for the individual learner; either the learner knows the answer or does not); (2) they expect immediate answers, and from an anybody-who-knows respondent; and (3) they word questions clumsily and cause the learners to wonder: "What does the teacher want?"

Adult students need questions that they can mull over and manipulate. They need questions that call for personal evaluation and judgment. Adults need time to ponder a reasonable response. (If the question is worth asking, it is worth fifteen to thirty seconds of thought time!)

Teachers need to involve learners in the questioning process, not simply the answering process. Asking questions may well show as much cognitive behavior as answering questions. Consider a "Circle of Questions." Put learners into a general circular configuration, assign each a verse or verses of the study text(s), and ask each to word a question based on his or her assigned content. Then proceed around the circle, letting each ask a question to the person to the left. (If your group could handle the consequence, don't let a learner ask a question until he or she has answered a question—to the satisfaction of the asker.) Continue around the circle until all questions are handled.

You could "prime" the group by distributing prepared questions. Consider First Timothy 3 as a text that lends itself to such a procedure. If you were distributing questions to learners, these could be useful:

First Timothy 3:1—"If *desire* is a true qualification for one becoming an 'overseer,' how does the church establish such desire?" 3:2—"What does it mean for an overseer to be 'above reproach'?" 3:3, 8—"Do the expressions 'not given to drunkenness' and 'not indulging in much wine' preclude any consumption of alcoholic drink?" 3:4, 5—"What is there about having his children obey him that has to do with being qualified for church leadership?" 3:6—How long does one need to be a confessed Christian before he is no longer a 'recent convert'?" 3:7—"How can the church establish that a candidate for the office of 'overseer has 'a good reputation with outsiders'? 3:9—"What does this verse/this trait actually mean?" 3:10—"How is one 'tested' to prove worthy to be a deacon?" 3:11—"Are the 'women' in this verse deacons' wives or female deacons?" 3:2, 12—"Does one have to be currently married (not widowed or divorced) to be 'faithful to his wife'?"

Asking questions is a time-honored strategy for successful teaching. Ask away!

MAPS AND CHARTS
Exploring the Geography and Chronology of the Bible

by James Riley Estep, Jr.

Stories that begin "Once upon a time" are just that—stories. We expect them to be fictional. The Bible, however, is not a book of fiction. Rather, it reflects the real history (chronology) of the real world (geography). Proper use of maps and charts will drive this fact home with your learners.

Most Bibles include a set of maps. So-called "Study Bibles" may go deeper in providing elaborate chronological charts. Often, these include not only the events recorded in the pages of Scripture, but also parallel events from secular history. The rise and fall of Egypt, Assyria, Babylon, etc., are important to the salvation-historical flow of the Bible narrative.

The problem, however, is that these maps and charts are so commonplace that we may take them for granted, forgetting their significance. Bible events intersect with other real-world events! This fact will strengthen our faith if approached properly.

Using Maps in Teaching Scripture

Many church classrooms have a set of Bible maps. But often it stands in a corner of the classroom untouched. They may be so old and frail that they are almost unusable. Here are three suggestions for using maps in Bible teaching.

1. Use large, colorful maps. I realize that some maps are in black-and-white and that some maps are designed for use on tabletops. But colorful maps that are visible from anywhere in your learning space will add to the learning experience, far more so than small, colorless ones.

2. Identify on the map movements and locations noted in the Bible text as your lesson progresses. Demonstrating the path of the exodus journey is an example. An inexpensive laser pointer works well for doing this. While you're at it, be sure to note the significance of locations that play more than one role in the Bible. For example, Bethlehem was not only the birthplace of Jesus, it was also the boyhood home of King David.

3. Project maps on a wall or screen. This is ideal for classrooms that do not have a set of maps or may be too large for a printed map to be seen from the back. You can do this in two ways. One

is to use digital mapping technologies. This will require a bit of an investment, but several software packages are available that have excellent map functions. One such package not only contains projectable Bible maps, but also allows the user to draw lines, circle items, and show distances with an automatic display. A cheaper, low-tech method is to use the overhead projector. Transparencies can be made by hand or by photocopying. Then it is easy to trace a journey or circle a city name with a marker.

Using Charts in Teaching Scripture

Charts include timelines, figures, and tables. Here are three suggestions for using charts in Bible teaching.

1. Use charts to explain. Concepts difficult to explain verbally may be grasped more easily by using a chart to clarify. A timeline of the period between the Old and New Testaments is an example.

2. Use charts to simplify. A chart can help your students comprehend a complicated subject that involves intersecting threads. A chart of the kings and prophets of Israel and Judah is an example.

3. Use charts to organize. A chart can help your learners see how a large mass of information fits together. For example, the Old Testament Jewish calendar is a dizzying mix of major and minor feasts, overlapping religious and civil calendars, unfamiliar month names, and Scripture references. Such information placed in a table of rows and columns will allow comprehension "at a glance."

Final Thoughts

Good teaching accounts for the fact that we live in a visual age. While maps and charts cannot replace Bible content, they can make that content memorable for your learners.

THE MEDIUM IS THE MESSAGE

Tapping the Power of Presentation Software

by Richard A. Koffarnus

The expression "the medium is the message" was coined by media expert Marshall McLuhan in his greatest work, *Understanding Media: The Extensions of Man (1964)*. Although frequently quoted, McLuhan's dictum is commonly misunderstood.

Many assume that McLuhan was (1) speaking strictly of mass-media communication and (2) that "the message" referred to the information presented by these media. Both assumptions are wrong. Worse yet, casual readers may conclude from these two assumptions that McLuhan was arguing that the content presented is less important than the medium that presents it. Nothing could be farther from the truth.

According to McLuhan, a *medium* is "any extension of ourselves." For example, a tennis racquet is a medium for extending my arm to the ball, and language is a medium for extending my thoughts to others. A *message*, on the other hand, is more than simply information. Ultimately, it is a change in human attitude or behavior in response to a medium. If I watch a video about evangelism in Haiti and feel compassion for the lost and decide to support a missionary to a third world country, then the message of the video is my change in attitude toward, and decision to support, missions.

Thus, when McLuhan says "the medium is the message," he means that the way to understand the nature of anything we create (a medium) and evaluate its effectiveness is by taking note of the changes it brings about (the message).

Bible School: Where the Medium Meets the Message

When you think about it, what you teach on Sunday morning is not a lesson; it's a group of students. The lesson is simply the medium by which you extend your thoughts and the truths of Scripture to them. The actual message is the change in your students' attitudes and actions that result from that lesson.

To help you maximize the desired effects of your lesson, publishers have begun including media tools as well as printed curriculum. Quite often what the publisher provides is a PowerPoint presentation to accompany the lesson. Standard Publishing provides such a presentation for every lesson in its Standard Lesson Quarterly curriculum (based on the Uniform Series). These Power-Point presentations are provided on the *Presentation Tools* CD that is included in the quarterly *Adult Resources* packet. Slide presentations can be copied to a hard drive, CD, or USB flash drive, or they can be shown directly from the CD. Additionally, Standard Publishing packages the *Adult Resources* packet, including the *Presentation Tools* CD, in its *Adult Teacher's Convenience Kit*. You also can get the PowerPoint presentations via download at www.standardlesson.com.

Of course, you don't have to rely on the publisher's presentation tools. You can make your own as well. This gives a personal touch that will be appreciated by your class. For that reason, it's a good idea to consider customizing publisher-provided presentations rather than simply using them as-is. Rephrase the discussion questions; include photos of people from your own church or scenes from your own city.

Putting the Power into PowerPoint

PowerPoint is a very flexible presentation program that mimics a slide projector on your computer. There was a time when a "slide show" usually meant a series of still pictures presented to a large crowd in a darkened auditorium. However, the use of PowerPoint in business and education has shown the versatility of the program in a variety of settings, from small group meetings to large congregations.

Unlike a slide projector, however, PowerPoint gives you the ability to change fonts and background color for each slide; to add pictures, clip art, animation, video clips, and music to slides; to rearrange slides; and much more—all at the click of a mouse.

In addition to your computer and the PowerPoint presentation, you will also need a means to display the presentation to your class. For a small group, a large screen monitor may be sufficient. The most flexible display solution, however, is a digital video projector and a projection screen. These are used increasingly in church worship services. Projectors vary widely in display resolution, light output, projection technology, and, accordingly, cost. So do your homework to be sure you get a projector that will meet your needs without breaking your budget.

Tapping the Potential of PowerPoint

If any medium is an extension of your thoughts, then think of a PowerPoint presentation as an extension of what you already do as a teacher. That poster you would use in a 10 x 12 classroom is now visible in a room three times as large. When you discuss a person or an event, you can project an applicable picture while you talk. Scripture references and quotations can be displayed while they are read aloud. In other words, whatever you say can be reinforced by what your class sees. And with PowerPoint you have the additional capability of printing copies of your slide program as handouts so your students can take the lesson home for further study and reflection.

If you prefer to use a discussion approach, as I do in my adult Bible class, you will find that displaying the questions will help stimulate discussion. When I ask a question in class, I sometimes get so involved in the discussion that I forget the original question. Having it displayed on screen can help me avoid a "senior moment." It can also be a useful tool to get the discussion back on track when a class member goes off on a tangent.

Avoiding Pitfalls

For all their power and pizzazz, slide shows often fizzle when it comes to the actual presentation. If you remember a few simple guidelines, however, you can avoid some common mistakes that may spoil your lessons.

First, keep the show brief. A common temptation is to pack too many slides into a single lesson. When that happens, the goal of the presentation can easily become to get through all the slides, rather than to drive home the life-changing message. Allow about one slide per minute of lesson time, and you won't feel rushed to finish.

Second, less is often more. One of the strengths of PowerPoint is also its greatest weakness. The program has a tempting array of tools that make it far too easy to have words and pictures fade in and out, bounce around the screen like rubber balls, and otherwise thoroughly distract the class. Unless your goal is to entertain, animation should be used to drive home an important point, not simply to amuse. Most of the slides on the *Adult Resources* CD have minimal animation or none at all so that they don't distract from the purpose of the lesson. Use the fireworks sparingly!

Third, keep it simple. Use few words and large letters or pictures on each slide so the class can easily recognize them in a large room. Too many words crammed on a slide make it difficult for the class to remember the content. Likewise, when you use bulleted points, limit the number of bullets to three or four per slide. Generally, sans serif fonts, such as Arial or Tahoma, are easier to read than serif, script, or decorative fonts.

Fourth, don't let the medium supersede the message. Marshall McLuhan argued that we should evaluate the effectiveness of any medium by its message, the change it brings about in its audience. Success is not measured by the "wow" factor of technology, but by its ability to help us achieve our goals. Even the most sophisticated slide show is still just a tool to reach your lesson objectives. As you see the lives of your students brought into conformity with the life of Jesus, then you will know that your teaching is having its desired effect.

PowerPoint Is Not the Only Option

While we have referenced PowerPoint repeatedly in this article, it's not the only such program available. Some would say it's not even the best option. But it does come with the Microsoft Office Suite that is preloaded on many new PCs, so it's extremely popular simply because it is available to so many people.

Apple makes a program called Keynote that some have found superior to PowerPoint—especially on the Macintosh platform. Google, the company behind the popular Internet search engine of the same name, also has a presentation software. Google Docs Presentation is gaining in popularity, especially with groups who design presentations collaboratively. It's also free, as are SlideRocket, 280Slides, and Prezi. Each of these has its adherents and detractors. You can research them and decide for yourself which you prefer.

Conclusion

Thanks to the influence of Christian writer G. K. Chesterton, Marshall McLuhan converted to the Christian faith in 1937. Thus, it is not surprising that after McLuhan's death in 1980 these words of Jesus were inscribed on his gravestone: "The Truth Shall Make You Free." When you couple the truth of God's Word with the power of presentation tools, the result can set your teaching—and your students—free, indeed.

Old and New, New and Old
Using Comparison and Contrast in Bible Teaching

by Ronald G. Davis

Struggling to describe or define objects or concepts often elicits comparisons and contrasts. Noting similarities and differences is one way we make sense of our world. Descriptions "draw a line around"—they say what is inside and what is not. Definitions "set the limits of"—something goes "this far" and no farther.

The use of comparison and contrast is always worthy of the teacher's consideration. Relating what students don't know to what they do know is good teaching. Some biblical texts employ this method, so it's natural for the teacher to adopt the method when teaching a lesson from one of those texts, but the creative teacher will find ways to use comparison and contrast on other types of material as well.

Texts from the epistle to the Hebrews adapt to this style easily. In this epistle we see the important similarities of the Old and New Covenants, but also the overwhelming difference: the absolute superiority of the New. The following text is a perfect example of the comparison/contrast strategy at work in teaching:

> In the past God spoke to our ancestors through the prophets at many times and in various ways, but in these last days he has spoken to us by his Son, whom he appointed heir of all things, and through whom also he made the universe. The Son is the radiance of God's glory and the exact representation of his being, sustaining all things by his powerful word. After he had provided purification for sins, he sat down at the right hand of the Majesty in heaven. (Hebrews 1:1-3)

God spoke "in the past"—when the Old Covenant was in force. He speaks "in these last days"—the era of the New Covenant. But now he is speaking not in words but in the *Word*. In the former days the speaking was of a temporary nature. In these last days the speaking is final: Jesus is God's last Word.

Using Similarities and Differences

Christianity is distinctively different from all the philosophies and pseudo religions of the world. The Christian has compared truth with lie, fact with theory, morality with pragmatism, evidence with supposition. He has concluded that Christian faith has superior answers to all of life's hard questions. True disciples persist in applying that same comparison/contrast mind-set to a wide range of circumstances.

Such an approach to teaching and learning offers several possibilities for in-class activity. One is the variety of *pen-and-paper activities* normally associated with tests and testing, which can call attention to important comparison/contrast elements in a lesson. Another is the use of *tables and charts*, which are essentially efforts to show how two or more concepts are alike and how they are different by highlighting shared and nonshared characteristics. A third involves *role playing*, which enables students to respond to hypothetical situations. This method is useful to emphasize the difference between Christian and non-Christian lifestyles and ways of thinking.

How well does the teacher of adults want his learners to know the Bible and its life-directing truths? The Spirit has spoken: "Until we all reach unity in the faith and in the knowledge of the Son of God. . . . We will no longer be infants, tossed back and forth by the waves, and blown here and there by every wind of teaching, . . . Instead, speaking the truth in love, we will grow to become in every respect the mature body of him who is the head, that is, Christ" (Ephesians 4:13-15).

Consider the following possibilities from the choices above and the texts suggested below:

True or False?

Tests generate thinking and demand choices. Thoughtful choice is at the heart of Christian faith. A narrative text such as Luke 24:36-53 lends itself to a test activity. To get learners to focus on the important facts of the text and to generate discussion of relevant issues, even a simple true-false test will work. As an example, take these ten statements taken from the text. The number in parentheses is the verse(s) where the answer to the statement can be found.

__ Jesus claimed to fulfill Scripture. (44, true)

__ The resurrected Christ had a fully human body. (39, true)

__ Doubt is impossible for true believers. (38, false)

__ Jesus ate food before his disciples to show them that he was not a spirit. (42, 43, true)

__ At his appearance, Jesus fully empowered his disciples. (49, false)

__ The disciples were deeply saddened at Jesus' ascension. (52, false)

__ The core elements of the gospel are Jesus' death and resurrection, and repentance and forgiveness. (46, 47, true)

__ The disciples never really worshiped Jesus. (52, false)

__ Jesus' initial words when he appeared to his disciples were, "Why are you not believing?" (36, false)

__ Jesus' final earthly deed was to bless his disciples. (50, 51, true)

Such a test is not designed simply to review and reinforce facts. Ponder the discussion possibilities. Key Christian doctrines—the deity of Christ and his bodily resurrection, for examples—are involved. Consider how the fellowship between Jesus and the disciples offers true encouragement to all who would be his today: he is concerned about our peace of mind; he trusts us to be his witnesses; he provides the joy of worship.

Whatever format you choose, a test can stimulate serious and significant reflection. Comparing truth with falsehood will move your learners toward the goals stated in Ephesians 4:13-15.

Side by Side

One simple but sure way to see the likenesses and the differences between two (or more) items is to hold them up side by side (by side). *Tables and charts*—whether on paper, chalkboard, or projected media—are designed to provide just such a view. In a vertical column, the items to be compared are named. In horizontal rows, the relevant characteristics are listed. Then the task is a simple: "Does this item have this particular characteristic or not?" Advertisers regularly use such a device to show the superiority of their product over comparable ones. They always highlight the advantages: "With the new Moxie sedan, leather seats are standard; in the Blahmobile, they're $650 extra!"

Paul used the same method in his message at Mars' Hill in Athens (Acts 17:22-34). Picture an imaginary chart with two headings: "Greek Gods" and "The Unknown God." Run through Paul's checklist as you read his sermon: (1) Made the world; (2) Lives in man-made temples; (3) Needs service from men; (4) Made every nation; (5) Expects men to repent; (6) Will judge the world; (7) Raised one from the dead; (8) Wants fellowship with men; (9) Made by man's design and skill; (10) Determines history with purpose. Some Athenians saw this comparison and sneered. Some wanted to hear more. A few became believers. The gospel always gets these responses. Thoughtful choices, based on comparison and contrast, will vary, but God always allows people to make their own choices.

Self or Others?

In certain ways Christian thinking and non-Christian thinking are alike. But at one significant point they differ greatly. "To serve or to be served"—that is the question. Christians exist to serve. Non-Christians exist to be served, so they think and act accordingly. The choice is self-centeredness or Christ-centeredness, being selfish or selfless. Jesus made it clear: "By this everyone will know that you are my disciples, if you love one another" (John 13:35). Non-Christians are likewise easily spotted: they love themselves.

The adult teacher will always have a desire to emphasize how the individual living under the New Covenant thinks and behaves differently from the ungodly. A lesson based on Matthew 18:1-4; 20:17-28 will provide a good occasion for pursuing that aim.

Role playing is one activity that allows students to experience tough choices without the risks of reality. (If one chooses poorly in a role play, the consequences are irrelevant.) For a lesson on the texts named above, class members might be assigned to be the Christian or non-Christian in each of the following hypothetical situations:

> You are driving carefully at the speed limit through a business district in the left lane, anticipating a left turn several blocks away. A car behind you accelerates, passes you on the right honking madly, and swerves dangerously close in front of you.

> As you leave the office after dark one evening, on the way to your car you are approached by a dirty, gaunt beggar asking, "Do you have a dollar for something to eat, friend?"

Ask your role players to dramatize and verbalize their responses. Have the group discuss whether the responses chosen reflect what the students would like to do or what they would really do. Through such an activity your learners should be challenged to "grow to become in every respect the mature body of him who is the head, that is, Christ" (Ephesians 4:15). What more worthy goal could Christian teachers have for their students?

ORGANIZING YOUR CLASS FOR LEARNING AND MINISTRY
Involving More People in Ministry

by Brett DeYoung

An adult class needs to have more people than just the teacher involved in its ministry. Too often the class is totally dependent on the teacher. This puts a tremendous amount of pressure on one person. It also leaves the class scrambling when that one person becomes sick, has to travel for work reasons, or for any other reason becomes unable to continue in that role.

Effective class organization not only relieves the teacher of stress, it also takes advantage of the giftedness of other class members. This can empower a class to reach out to newcomers, meet the needs in the lives of its members, and become an example of a group working together to grow in discipleship.

Consider the following descriptions for an adult class ministry team.

Teacher

1. Teaches the class each week or provides a suitable substitute.
2. Plans the curriculum for each quarter.
3. Helps advertise the class through church publicity.
4. Meets with the class ministry team.
5. Provides spiritual leadership and vision for the class.

Co-Teacher (or Regular Substitute)

A co-teacher will work alongside the teacher in a team-teaching role. As such, this person will be involved in the same things the teacher is (above), though usually in an apprentice-type role. The co-teacher will mostly perform tasks as assigned by the teacher, but the intent should be that this person will one day become the teacher of the class (or another class). A regular substitute will work with the teacher to a lesser degree. He or she will need to be aware of the teaching plan and available to fill in when the teacher is not able to teach. Either the co-teacher or regular substitute should attend meetings of the class ministry team.

Class Leader

1. Organizes meetings and duties of the class ministry team.

2. Coordinates the nonteaching portions of the class (i .e., prayer concerns, announcements). This person typically will open and close each class meeting, being sure to guard a reasonable amount of time for the teacher's segment.

3. Organizes the selection and recruitment of class ministry team members.

4. Leads the effort to meet any special needs of the class not related to the shepherding ministry. (See below.) For example, some churches meet in temporary quarters; others have multiple services and multiple classes using the same room. In either case, someone may need to organize the setup and takedown of the classroom.

5. Helps set policies for class organization.

6. In the absence of a co-teacher or regular substitute, this person may be the substitute teacher when the teacher is ill or traveling.

Social Director

1. Plans and organizes the class socials. Some classes have these monthly; others find a quarterly schedule works better. At least one or two of these each year should be a ministry or service event and not just fellowshipping with the "regulars."

2. Coordinates the social activities with the church calendar.

3. Coordinates the refreshments brought to class each week. This does not mean this person always provides the refreshments, but he or she makes sure someone is taking care of it. It may be as simple a thing as putting out a sign-up sheet for people to volunteer to bring something in.

4. Provides publicity and announcements for social events.

Shepherding Director

1. Helps develop and update a class roster to keep track of the attendance of class members.

2. Develops a follow-up ministry to contact members who are absent for more than two weeks. Some classes only follow up on absences when the reason for a person's absence is not known. This becomes (or is perceived as) a process of "checking up" on "delinquent" members. It's better if all absences are followed up on. If a member has been traveling, how nice to return home to find a card from the class saying "Welcome home" or "We've been praying for safe travels." If the member is sick, regular get-well cards and "We're praying for you cards" are great encouragement. If this is routine, then the occasional "We're praying for you" or "We missed you" to the student absent without cause is no surprise and more likely to have positive results.

3. Notifies the class leader and teacher of special needs (absences, prayer, benevolence, etc.).

4. Enlists other class members to assist in the shepherding ministry.

5. Helps organize the care for special needs of the class, such as meals to the sick, ministry in times of grief, baby showers, and other special events.

Secretary/Treasurer

1. Counts the number of students in the class and keeps a weekly attendance record. Reports multiple absences to the shepherding director.

2. Collects and records offerings. (Some churches require offerings to be turned in to the Sunday school office or church office. Be sure to work with the church leadership to make sure any collecting of monies for the class's use is done in a proper manner.)

3. Disburses funds with the approval of the class or class ministry team.

4. Reports the financial status at the class meetings.

Missions/Outreach Director

1. Enlists people to welcome and introduce visitors to the class.

2. Develops a system to involve visitors in the activities of the class.

3. Regularly gets names from the church staff of potential class members, adults who attend worship but are not involved in the Sunday school. This includes visitors, new members, and long-time worship-only attenders. Make sure these people get invited to the class and to class socials. Include them when considering families who need special ministry. Just as you might take meals in to the home of a sick class member, do the same for potential class members who do not have a class to that for them.

4. Helps develop service projects for class involvement.

5. Helps select a mission opportunity for class support.

Meetings of the Class Ministry Team

On some regular basis, quarterly at least, the class leader should hold a meeting of the entire class ministry team. Here you can share details of the class needs—who is sick, who is traveling, who needs prayer, who needs additional ministry, etc. You can also talk about upcoming lessons and lesson themes. The social director can use that information to make the next social more relevant. The outreach director can include some of that information in inviting potential members. This becomes a time for coordinating the efforts of all the team members so that the class functions as a unit. It's not all business. It's a lot of ministry, too, as the needs of members are prayed about and plans are made to address the needs.

Classes who do not have ministry teams put a lot of responsibility in the hands of one person: the teacher. The class becomes something like a one-man band. Some one-man bands are pretty good; they bring a lot of laughs when they perform at the circus. But how much better is the performance of the symphony orchestra or the university marching band that performs at halftime! Which would you rather hear?

PUT IT IN WRITING

How Writing Can Help Students Learn and Apply Bible Truths

by Ronald G. Davis

Written words stand stark and demanding on the page. When they are personalized, they call for attention and response. That is the nature of God's written Word: "O child, I love you. I want the very best for you—for eternity! Obey me." All the words that his Spirit moved men to write are to that end.

Paul's letters are just such written, Spirit-inspired words—"able to make you wise for salvation . . . useful for teaching, rebuking, correcting and training in righteousness" (2 Timothy 3:15, 16). Words spoken orally carry all the power and authority of the one who speaks; words in print carry that plus the permanence that allows pondering and personalizing. God "spoke to our ancestors" long ago (Hebrews 1:1), and he also had his words secured in print. Through the written Word of God, we know the mind of God—his love and grace, his holiness and judgment.

Three Opportunities

Adult teachers will want to take advantage of this phenomenon in instructing their learners. The mind of the learner heard in speech is important; the mind of the learner seen in print adds one more dimension to the teaching-learning bond. The perceptive teacher will examine every lesson text closely for an opportunity for learners to put pen to paper.

Three ingredients of the successful lesson offer an opportunity to have the learners write something: first, helping them see exactly what the text says; second, helping them understand what the text means; and third, helping them put God's truth to work in daily living. So get your adults to "Put It in Writing."

What Does It Say?

One easy way to get started is to have the class create a simple "test" based on the lesson text. Assign each member a verse of the text (or two verses, or two students to a verse) and ask that he write a true-false statement that can be answered by his assigned verse(s).

Colossians 1:15-29 will serve as an example text. Look at sample possibilities from verses 15 and 16 alone. Verse 15: "In a certain sense, Jesus is the firstborn of/over all creation" (true); "Jesus is obviously lower than God for he is 'the image of the invisible God' and 'the firstborn of every creature'" (false). Verse 16: "Jesus was an active, full participant in creation" (true); "Every element of creation can be viewed by the human eye" (false); "Creation was not only *by* Jesus but *for* Jesus" (true).

When they are finished, each student can stand randomly and read his or her statement, anticipating that others will respond with "true" or "false" or with the relevant verse number. Or collect all the statements, shuffle them, and then give the "test" to the entire class. (The latter approach may remove some of the intimidation that certain members may have about speaking in class.)

An even simpler approach to a text is to ask class members to characterize a text by its key words or key ideas. An index card is large enough to use for this kind of activity. Tell each student to select three or four words that best characterize a particular lesson text and its ideas.

Ephesians 4:1-16 will serve well as an example. The fact that the text includes a number of repeated words and a dominant theme lends itself to such an activity. Ask the class to write down three words that characterize the text. When they have finished, ask the class to send their lists around the room simultaneously—establish a "circular" pattern for the passing—and after all lists have circulated, ask the group to identify the "most common" words and the "most uncommon" words. (You may find an idea that is not clear or obvious to some members; stop and ask the one who made the suggestion to explain his or her choice.) Some words that you might expect to be "common" from Ephesians 4 include *one, unity, Christ, love, gifts,* and *maturity;* some words that might appear but are unlikely to be as prevalent are *teaching, body,* and *measure.* The similarities and differences in such lists will provide an excellent overview of the contents and emphases of many texts.

What Does It Mean?

Once a student sees what a text says, the next step of his study must be to obtain its true and proper meaning. The revelation of Scripture is, by God's design, clear and concise. With most texts, the expectations of God are obvious (sometimes uncomfortably so). But because the historical setting of the Bible was "far away and long ago," because the words were originally penned in languages other than English, and because both scholars and the unlettered have sometimes distorted their intent, every text must be examined with the question, "What does this mean?" The teacher should examine every lesson text to anticipate how it might appear unclear and how to help the learner adjust the lens of his mind to bring the "image" into focus.

Paraphrasing thoughts is a helpful approach to clarifying and understanding them. Ask students to prepare paraphrases of part or all of a given lesson text. (A bonus is that such paraphrases may indicate certain students have serious misunderstandings of the text and provide occasion for correction.)

As the teacher, you may need to give examples to get your class started in the practice of paraphrasing. Philemon provides a worthy text for such an activity. Verse 22 includes Paul's final request before his closing greetings; his words might be paraphrased as follows: "Philemon, I know you've been praying for me to be free to come and visit—get a room ready!"

Once again, assign a verse (or pairs of verses that contain a single thought) to each class member. Simply say, "Put this in your own words." Some may choose to place the message in a contemporary setting; others will personalize it. Allow them that freedom. Challenge all of your students to attempt to capture the emotion—the heart—of the assigned text.

Final products of this assignment can be collected, in verse order, and then read consecutively as listeners compare their efforts with the Bible text. Or you could shuffle the paraphrases and read them randomly, asking your students to match each paraphrase with the corresponding Bible verse.

How Do I Put This Truth to Work?

Most adults "know" all sorts of truths that often have no real impact on their lives. The adult teacher's ultimate goal is that no Bible truth is left in the mind of his learners without being "translated" into godly behavior.

Many lessons lend themselves to application through writing personal notes of encouragement and edification. Occasionally the adult learner needs to write a commitment statement for his own edification, which can then serve as a daily challenge to right thinking, speaking, and living.

For example, give your class a completion statement to finish as a challenge for the coming days. Suggest that they keep this with them or display it prominently as a regular reminder. For a lesson from Philippians 2 you might have the learners complete and carry this statement: "Lord, in lowliness of mind, this week I will esteem _____ better than myself, and I will demonstrate that by. . . ." (See Philippians 2:3.) For a lesson from Philippians 4, try, "Lord, I'm exhausted by my anxiety over _____; I turn this matter over to you." (See Philippians 4:6.) For a lesson from Ephesians 2 dare the class to affirm, "Lord, I know that I have been 'created in Christ Jesus to do good works'; therefore, I will . . ." (See Ephesians 2:10.)

However, the more significant writing that a student can do in putting truth to work is that which he does for another: to build up a sister or brother in Christ or to offer Christ's good news to one who is suffocating under the pile of the world's (and the devil's) bad news.

To every adult with a living parent, the words from Ephesians 5 and 6 are timely. The simple reminder, "Honor your father and mother" (6:2), and the earlier command to "follow God's example . . . as dearly loved children" (5:1) should strike a responsive chord. What parent would not be honored to receive a loving note, a phone call, a gift, or a visit from an adult daughter or son? The adult teacher should provide the incentive (even the stationery and postage if need be) for this activity.

Finally, for every adult student and every adult teacher, there is surely that friend or acquaintance who needs the good news of Christ. Another way to put truth to work is by giving it the opportunity to work in someone else!

PUTTING THE EM'·PHA·SIS ON THE RIGHT SYL'·LA·BLE

by Ronald G. Davis

Emphasis. That is what writer and speaker strive for. God's Spirit certainly knows emphasis. So, much of God's Word is written in emphatic form and style. Poetic style, in which much of the Bible is presented, is always emphatic.

In poetry there is the emphasis of repetition. This is especially true of Hebrew poetry's emphatic parallelism. But there is also the emphasis of figurative language that manages to say something twice with one set of words. The figurative stirs a thought of recognition and application.

A Christian teacher of adults will at times wisely choose poetry and poetic activity to follow in the Spirit's train. And every such teacher wants the educational emphasis of ideas that such choices allow. Consider the following learning activities related to figurative language, parallelism, and poetry.

A Favorite Poem

To get class members involved in a course of study from one of the Bible's poetic books, establish a display board for verses that are related to the studies. Put the title of this article as the title of your display. At the first study, or even a week or two before, give your class members a list of the primary themes of the study. Say, "You probably have one or more favorite poetic verses that relate to our coming studies. I have put up this board for a display. Bring them in week to week, and we will all enjoy them."

Next distribute the list of themes that you will be following. For example, you might have the following (from a past quarter of the Uniform Series: "The Glory of God's Creation," "Living with Creation's Uncertainties," and "Lessons in Living." You can add key phrases such as *Praise, God's Presence, Hope, Resurrection, Meaning, Times and Seasons, Wisdom and Success, Integrity and Shame, and Godly Women and Family*. Suggest sources such as hymn lyrics, classic poems from school curriculum, greeting cards, and even class members' own compositions.

You may wish to post a few samples to get the activity started. Consider the following, a traditional song about the sadness and futility of life without God and Jesus. This would work well in a study of Ecclesiastes, in which Solomon bemoans the futility and discouragement of life "under the sun."

> *How Tedious and Tasteless*
> How tedious and tasteless, the hours
> When Jesus I no longer see;
> Sweet prospects, sweet birds, and sweet flowers,
> Have all lost their sweetness to me.
>
> . . . .
>
> O drive these dark clouds from the sky,
> Thy soul cheering presence restore;
> Or take me to thee up on high,
> Where winter and clouds are no more.

A simple poem such as Emily Dickinson's "I'm Nobody! Who Are You?" could well reflect an attitude in contrast with David's expression of Psalm 8:4: "What is mankind that you [God] are mindful of them?" Such a poem as E. E. Cummings's "i thank you God for most this amazing" is a beautiful expression of praise, certainly appropriate for Psalm 104 or a similar passage.

Further, one can hardly hear Job's humble acknowledgement of God's sovereignty and care in Job 42 and not remember the powerful confession of Civilla Martin's words: "Why should I feel discouraged, why should the shadows come, / Why should my heart be lonely, and long for heaven and home, / When Jesus is my portion? My constant Friend is he: / His eye is on the sparrow, and I know he watches me"? And the hymnal is also a certain source of poems extolling the resurrection and its power.

Just a Couplet

Two-line poetic expressions are among the first that children learn to chant, and they still intrigue the adult. When studying a passage that is written in the parallelism common to Hebrew writers, encouraging your adults to express themselves similarly is a worthy goal.

In Psalm 8 each verse is a typical example of an expression followed by a related expression—sometimes a simple restatement in other words. For such a lesson, consider asking your students to complete the first expression with a second of their own composition. Verse 1 begins, "Lord, our Lord, how majestic is your name in all the earth!" The couplet could be completed with an expression such as, "May your name be praised by all," etc.

Consider selecting a first expression from verses such as the following and asking class members to complete them: Psalm 8:6; Psalm 104:5; Psalm 139:7; Psalm 145:13; Job 1:21; Job 32:8; Job 42:2; Ecclesiastes 1:4; Ecclesiastes 3:14; Proverbs 3:5; Proverbs 8:5; Proverbs 11:12; Proverbs 31:26.

(While this list comes from an actual quarter of studies, you could select the texts from your own course of study.) This exercise could be the assignment as students arrive or could be the homework for a lesson to come. Later comparisons and contrasts with the Bible text will emphasize the truth of the selected verses.

It Figures

An important part of poetic expression is the careful choice of figures of speech. Robert Frost emphasized the importance of simple decisions in the course of life in "The Road Not Taken" by using the figure of a fork in the road. Similarly the proverb writer personifies wisdom (Proverbs 8:1), and Job compares a life to a flower (Job 14:2). The comparative device of figurative language is powerful.

The teacher's device can be as simple as beginning a comparison and letting class members complete it. For example, in a study of Psalm 8 try, "Man is like a . . . " Such similes allow not only a discussion of similarities but also demand a discussion of differences, such as the psalmist does when he says, "made them a little lower than the angels" (Psalm 8:5). In Proverbs 31, the writer says of the godly woman that "strength and dignity" are her clothing. Having the students examine the text for other articles of her "clothing" would prove profitable. For example, do not several verses speak of her skill in household crafts? Does not verse 20 show generosity and kindness hanging in her "wardrobe"? Let your adults think creatively of her whole "closet."

Child's Play

Involving children in the adult classroom offers real interest and variety. A class member's child or grandchild presenting a short and simple children's poem to the adult class can provoke true discussion of the significant themes from the Scriptures.

Though one might think children's poems are all fluff and nonsense, the great children's poets tackle the real issues of a child's life: feelings, hopes, life, and death. In the collections of such children's poets as David McCord, Aileen Fisher, Karla Kuskin, John Ciardi, Arnold Adoff, Jack Prelutsky, Shel Silverstein, and others, deep thoughts are expressed in humor and in deep sensitivity. (If you have an elementary school teacher or former one in your class, that person may relish finding "just the right poem" and inviting "just the right child" to read or say it to your class.)

In only 32 words Langston Hughes calls vividly for the hope only "Dreams" can sustain. Texts from Job and other Scriptures can be illuminated by such imagery. Christina Rossetti (1830–1894) captures the wonder of creation that the psalmist extols; hear her "Who Has Seen the Wind?":

Who has seen the wind?
Neither I nor you:
But when the leaves hang trembling,
The wind is passing through.

Who has seen the wind?
Neither you nor I:
But when the trees bow down their heads,
The wind is passing by.

For a lesson on integrity, a reading/singing of the stanzas of "I Would Be True" by Howard A. Walter can add impact at application time. Having two alternating readers/speakers will add to the impact. For a lesson from Psalm 104, a child's reading Calvin Miller's "Catherine Caterpillar" from his book of children's poems *When the Aardvark Parked on the Ark* can emphasize the marvel of God's plans for each of his creatures.

Wax Poetic

God's Spirit often waxed poetic when he wanted to reveal God and his will. The beauty, the emphasis, the thought-provoking value of those expressions in the Word are a strong challenge to the teacher of Christian adults: how can I follow in his example? Give poetry a chance, and it will weave its web of power over your students.

PUZZLERS, POSERS, AND PROPHECIES:

Understanding the Mystery

by Ronald G. Davis

Light reveals that which otherwise would be hidden in darkness. God's will would have been just such a hidden matter unless he had given light. Human observation can discover some basic doctrines about God (see Romans 1:18-32), but his scheme of redemption had to be revealed. Only when he gave light could people know his will and way. Often that light came in small amounts, piquing interest and creating a yearning to know more.

The Christian teacher has the same purpose: giving light so that people can know, understand, believe, and practice God's will. And the teacher may fulfill that purpose in the same way that God often did: as if it were a riddle to be answered, a coded message to be deciphered. God's messianic prophecies were just such puzzles—they needed that one last piece God would provide; Jesus' parables were just such enigmas—they needed his spiritual explanation and the listener's purity of spirit to be fully comprehended. Both had the same two requirements to be successful: adequate revelation from God and mental attention and diligence on the part of the learner.

Bible lesson material that is essentially non-narrative in style may well lend itself to a variety of puzzles and word games enjoyed by adults. The focus required and the joy of discovery are learning processes the teacher of adults longs to see. Lessons from the sometimes cryptic book of Isaiah accommodate themselves to several word puzzles.

Five Key Words

A series of lessons from Isaiah might suggest some of the blessings God's Servant brings: light, peace, comfort, hope, and justice. (Other key words might also be chosen, and there could be more or fewer than five. For the sake of example, however, we'll use these five key words.) The adult teacher might use one or more of the following activities to emphasize those blessings.

The popularity of the game show "Wheel of Fortune" makes a basic "fill-in-the-blank" activity a good possibility.

G__D'__   __ER__ANT   __R__NG__   __ __G__T,__EA__E,   __ __ __ __ __RT,
__ __ __ E, AND __ __ __T__ __ E.

(Solution: *"God's servant brings light, peace, comfort, hope, and justice."*)

One might use a simple list of the five words scrambled.

G H I L T	(light)
A C E E P	(peace)
C F M O O R T	(comfort)
E H O P	(hope)
C E I J S T U	(justice)

Many adults will enjoy a word find puzzle.

E	C	I	T	S	U	J	G	E	C	I	T	S	U	J	G
E	P	O	H	O	D	S	S	E	P	O	H	O	D	S	S
E	E	R	M	V	A	N	L	E	E	R	M	V	A	N	L
T	A	G	O	F	D	S	I	T	A	G	O	F	D	S	I
S	C	E	R	V	O	A	G	S	C	E	R	V	O	A	G
N	E	T	G	O	D	R	H	N	E	T	G	O	D	R	H
S	S	E	R	V	A	N	T	S	S	E	R	V	A	N	T

A letter substitution code is a little more challenging. In the following example, learners may quickly figure out the five words, but ask them to deduce the nature of the code. (Each letter in the original word is replaced by the letter that comes after it in the alphabet by the same number of spaces as the original letter's position in the word. That is, the first letter is replaced by the first letter after it, the second by the second letter after, etc.)

M K J L Y	(light)
Q G D G J	(peace)
D Q P J T X A	(comfort)
I Q S I	(hope)
K W V X N I L	(justice)

Another fun code hides words in back-to-back words (or within a word) in unrelated sentences:
1. What a de**light**ful experience we had at the church picnic! (*light* in "delightful")
2. We ho**pe a ce**ntury is long enough to wait. (*peace* in "hope a century")

3. Go to "Bible.com" for the best Bible commentary on the web. (*comfort* in "Bible.com for the")

4. We must accept the Servant with open hearts. (*hope* in "with open")

5. If just I cede my property rights, will the church survive? (*justice* in "just I cede")

Words and Ideas, Ideas and Words

With a series of lesson texts in which lists of attributes are predominant, the adult teacher will want to consider the variety of puzzle-type language activities that can highlight and reinforce those characteristics, whether they be desirable traits for God's servants, demeaning sins of God's people, or objective descriptors of God's leaders.

Consider such a simple activity for a lesson from Isaiah 49:1-61. Give the learners a list of descriptors of Israel, and ask the class to identify how each is seen in the text. Use this list (or one of your own compilation): *chosen, purposive, beloved, disappointing, prepared (i.e., gifted), glorious, strengthened, privileged, powerful.*

For a lesson from Isaiah 11:1-9, consider doing an "A-B-C search"; that is, ask the learners to devise words for as many letters of the alphabet as possible, based in some fashion on the text, that describe the Coming One

Here are possibilities and verse references/explanations:

A: all-knowing (2); **B**: branch (1); **C**: counselor (2); **D**: destroyer (4);

E: equalizer (will make things right, v. 4); **F**: fearful (3); **G**: __;

H: human (son of Jesse, v. 1); **I**: insightful (3, 4); **J**: just (3, 4); **K**: king (1-9);

L: Lord (9); **M**: Messiah (anointed by the Spirit, v. 2);

N: noble (of high birth and possessing outstanding characteristics, vv. 1-9);

O: __; **P**: powerful (slays with his words, v. 4); **Q**: quick (3); **R**: righteous (5);

S: Spirit-filled (2); **T**: transformer (6-8); **U**: unlimited (3); **V**: victorious (9);

W: well-known (9); **X**: __; **Y**: __; **Z**: __.

The range of responses any learning group will devise will offer much opportunity to discuss and even disagree. (And some of your students will devise words for the blank letters above!) Or as teacher you can display such a list and ask learners to identify a verse or verses that reveal the attribute.

A lesson from Isaiah 40, with its figurative language, lends itself to an activity called "Object Match." In this activity various objects that are designed to reflect phrases, words, and ideas from the text are displayed. Learners match the objects to verses of the text. Consider this list for verses 1-11: a quilted comforter (v. 1); a (toy) sword or gun (v. 2); a megaphone (v. 3); a cactus (v. 3); a contorted chenille wire (v. 4); sandpaper (v. 4b); tall cut grass (v. 6); wildflower—real or artificial (v. 6b); a hardcover Bible that can be stood up, (v. 8b); a newspaper (v. 9); a carpenter's rule (v. 10); a stuffed toy lamb (v. 11). The objects could be displayed all at once, letting learners identify verses at random, or each object can be revealed at its own time, asking learners to identify a relevant verse and connection.

Thoughtworthy

Lessons from the book of Ruth are ideal study material for the one who would be godly. The book is indeed "thoughtworthy." The Spirit, by the pen of Paul, advised all to think on certain things that are in themselves of the nature of God: things that are true, noble, right, pure, lovely, admirable, excellent, or praiseworthy (Philippians 4:8). The teacher can, by asking learners to label lessons and texts with these eight characteristics, help them to understand how the Bible helps them to think godly thoughts, even when the lessons or texts emphasize ungodly behaviors.

One way to do this is to post the verse (Philippians 4:8) with the eight attributes highlighted. Then ask the class members to examine the text for examples of any of the "thoughtworthy" characteristics. For example, in a lesson from Ruth 1, the judges existed (v. 1) to see that justice was honored; Elimelech's move of his family at a time of famine (v. 2) is certainly noble; God's revisiting Israel with the blessing of food (v. 6) is certainly praiseworthy; Naomi's prayer for her daughters-in-law to be blessed by the Lord (v. 8) is lovely indeed; and the heartfelt appeal of Ruth to accompany Naomi (vv. 16, 17) demonstrates a rare purity of motive. Asking learners to write the eight attributes into appropriate places into a printed copy of the text, before group discussion, may be a preferable approach. If you have an "active" class, ask eight learners to sit across the front of your room; assign to each of them one of the traits; and ask them to "pop" up whenever their attributes are referred to as the Scripture text is read. As each stands, stop and ask, "Why did you stand?" Having them hold labels can enhance learning.

"Figuring out" truth from clues and symbols is thinking at a higher level. Adults who enjoy the challenge of a daily newspaper crossword puzzle or cryptogram will find similar challenges in comparable activities in the Bible study classroom. The perceptive and committed teacher of adults will offer the challenge.

REACHING EVERY LEARNER
One Size Doesn't Fit All

by Wendy Guthrie

Walk into the average adult Sunday school class and you will find a group of adults sitting in chairs (usually three or four rows deep) listening to a lecturer. Now this is not necessarily a bad thing, but it does assume that every member of that class learns in the same way—which just isn't true.

The apostle Paul reminds us of each member's uniqueness when he uses the analogy of "many members" in "one body" (Romans 12:4). Paul was referring specifically to the giftedness of each member and his or her place in service to the church. By extension, we can apply the "many" idea to the learning styles of the students who sit in your Sunday school class. Students take in and process information in different ways. Marilee B. Sprenger proposes that there are four types of learners.

Four Types of Learners

The *imaginative learner* is people-oriented. She learns through emotions; she trusts her perceptions. This learner needs dialogue in order to process information and is most interested in how the content of the lesson applies to her personal life. She wants to know the value of the lesson, so her favorite question is "Why?"

The *analytic learner* is knowledge-oriented. He needs information, and lots of it. This learner thrives in the lecture format. He is a sponge that soaks up the information and then needs time to process it and reflect on it. This learner thinks logically and analyzes content before he is ready to do anything with it; his favorite question is "What?"

The *common-sense learner* is solution-oriented. She needs to put her knowledge into action. This learner is a pragmatist; she doesn't need much time to think through material, and she processes information better if it is hands-on. This learner is most interested in the usefulness of the lesson material, so her favorite question is "How?"

The *dynamic learner* is discovery-oriented. He sees the world differently from most; he is the visionary. This learner takes in information through all of his senses and processes it through his actions.

He likes to "think outside the box" and try things that "have never been done that way." This learner is most interested in what the lesson content could become, so his favorite question is "What if?"

As you read through the characteristics, I'm sure you found the one that best describes you. However, I'm also sure you said "Well, that could be me" about one or two other learning styles. Thus the four styles are not "air tight." In his infinite wisdom, God has placed aspects of these various learning styles within each of us. That means we all need lessons that meet the criteria above if we are going to be the disciples Christ has called us to be.

The Learning Cycle

Right about now you may be tempted to throw your hands up in surrender and say, "I have only 45 minutes for a lesson; how can I possibly address everyone's learning needs in that amount of time?" Let me assure you it's not as hard as it seems. By following a learning cycle called *4MAT*, developed by Bernice McCarthy, any teacher can meet the needs of every learning style in the class.

The cycle has distinct phases. First, you must connect the lesson to students in some way that makes them want to learn. When you have done this, students will attend to the specifics of the lesson in order to derive value from it. At this point, students are ready for the underlying theories and are able to imagine or conceptualize them.

Then comes the time to inform students of the facts of the lesson. (This is the part of the cycle with which most teachers feel most comfortable.) After students know what the lesson says, they're ready to practice or master that information.

But the lesson cannot stop there. Students also need to know how to extend the information outside of the classroom. They will need to refine it so it fits the needs of the community. Finally, they need to perform or put it into action so it makes a difference in someone's life.

The best way to make sure your lessons reach students in each of these phases is to ask yourself the following questions:

- How will your students connect with the lesson? *(connect)*
- How do you plan to deliver the lesson content? *(inform)*
- How do you plan for your students to practice the content? *(practice)*
- How will they examine or reflect on their experience? *(attend)*
- How will your students apply this lesson to their lives? *(extend)*
- In what ways will your students need to critique and modify the lesson for application? *(refine)*
- How can your students share what they have developed with others? *(perform)*
- How well do your students understand everything that has happened in the lesson? *(imagine)*

Creating the Lesson

Once you've wrestled with these questions, you're ready to turn the answers into a lesson. Here's how you could develop a lesson from Leviticus 8:1-13 using the 4MAT system:

1. Retell the details of the dedication of Aaron's family for special service to God and the community; help learners understand the principle of being dedicated for service; encourage individuals to accept roles of special service and to recognize persons called for service.

2. Summarize the details of the text and write them on strips of poster board (one concept per strip). Have students read the passage to themselves and then work as a group to put the strips in the correct order.

3. Have students work in small groups to plan a Sunday school teacher dedication service. Make sure the groups translate the principles from the Scripture text into their services.

4. Ask students to recap a dedication or installation service they attended.

5. Have students reflect on what made the service in #4 special. Connect their remarks with the principles from the lesson text.

6. Have one or more groups volunteer to work with the Sunday school superintendent (or other leader) to plan a teacher dedication service prior to the kick-off of the next "curriculum year" (typically in the fall).

7. Have students brainstorm ideas about having dedication or installation services for those who perform other tasks in the church.

8. Have students take a spiritual gifts inventory to determine their spiritual strengths. Then have each student identify at least two areas of service they could perform within the church that would enable them to use their spiritual gifts.

9. Have students identify some guiding principles from the lesson text that could apply to ceremonies within the church today. (This activity will need to follow the one in #2 above.)

Once you establish the various activities that can be used in the lesson, the next step is to organize them into a plausible order for the lesson. The nice thing about the 4MAT system is that you don't have to organize the lesson in the same way every Sunday. Some days you may want to start with the text, while other Sundays you may want to start by having students connect with the lesson topic.

One possible order for this lesson is to begin by having students recap a dedication service they attended (#4) and then explain what made it special (#5). From that point you can move right into the Scripture by having students arrange the lesson events in the correct order (#2); then formulate overriding principles from the text (#9).

This naturally leads into the application phase of the lesson by asking students to prepare a "mock" dedication service using the principles from the previous activity (#3). Extend that activity by asking students to brainstorm similar services they could design (#7).

It's important to make sure that applications that begin in the classroom make it outside the door. Having students volunteer to organize a teacher dedication service based on the class activity (#6) is one way to accomplish this. Suggest that students complete a spiritual gifts inventory on a Web site such as www.churchgrowth.org; they can use the results to commit themselves to greater service within the local body (#8).

Conclusion

If you use the 4MAT system, be prepared for students to take notice. The *imaginative learners* will now engage in conversation that relates to the lesson rather than conversation that distracts others. The *common-sense learners* will be motivated to put hands and feet to their faith. The *dynamic learners* will no longer feel like misfits because your class will encourage them to cast the vision for everyone else. The *analytic learners* will still be sitting on the front row taking in every word.

The important thing to remember is that learners are more in tune when the lesson is relevant. The best way to make a lesson relevant is for you to stay in tune with the learning styles of your students.

READY, AIM, TEACH
The Importance of Lesson Aims in Teaching

by Jonathan Underwood

Do you ever wonder whether you are doing any good as the teacher of your class? Does it ever seem you are just passing time in class instead of accomplishing anything meaningful? If so, perhaps you need to take a second look at the lesson aims (also called learning goals) in your lesson. In the *Standard Lesson Commentary* and *Standard Lesson Quarterly* teacher books, these aims are carefully crafted to get you started on the right path and to keep you focused on your goal. (If your curriculum does not spell out the lesson aims, then it's important that you, the teacher, take time to identify your own goals for each lesson.)

Where Are You Going?

Someone has said, "If you don't know where you are going, then any road will take you there." To know which is the right road, or the right way, one must know where he or she wants to be. The same is true in teaching. Unless you have a clear idea of what you want to accomplish by the end of the class session—where you want your students to be, if you please—then there is no way to know just what you ought to spend your time doing in the class session.

What is your goal in teaching? Surely it is more than providing sixty minutes worth of diversion; you're not just filling time. And you're not just trying to cover a particular portion of Scripture. No, you want more. You want your students to know something they may not have known before they came into your classroom. More than that, you want them to understand the truths and principles of Scripture that the lesson text presents. Finally, you want the students to apply to their lives those things they have come to know and understand. In other words, you have a "content" aim, a "concept" aim, and a "conduct" aim.

The Content Aim: "What does the text say?"

This aim addresses the issue of what facts the student should know as a result of having participated in the study of the assigned lesson text. Verbs like *recount, tell*, and *identify* will frequently introduce such aims. Knowledge of Bible content is foundational.

The Concept Aim: "What does the text mean?"

The second aim is a concept aim. This goal probes beneath the surface of the material to find the timeless principles underlying the facts reported in the Scripture text.

This aim takes the learner beyond the knowledge of facts toward understanding. This is a necessary link to bring the historical truth about events of centuries gone by to relevance to learners in our own day. Verbs like *relate, compare,* and *explain* will be more common in introducing these aims.

The Conduct Aim: "What does the text demand of me?"

The third aim is a conduct aim. This is the goal that addresses the issue of application: How will the students' conduct change as a result of participating in this study? Such aims may challenge the learner to make a commitment or to suggest a specific action that he or she can take in the coming week. Action verbs dominate this aim: *write, help, do*, and other words of action.

Putting It Together

So, are any of the three aims more important than the other two? Or are all three equally important? What you as the teacher choose to stress depends on the nature of the lesson you're teaching.

The concept aims are especially important, for example, in studying the historical narratives in Scripture. It is not enough to know the facts about the story of David's killing the giant Goliath. We must also understand the principles of faith and courage that moved David to action. Only then can we move on from the content aim, knowing the facts, to the conduct aim: applying this lesson to how we face the giants in our own lives. In some passages, especially in the epistles, the content may be more exposition than narration, more conceptual than historical. In these cases we may find that to know the content of the passage is almost the same as knowing the concept.

Thus, starting your lesson preparation with a clear understanding of what you want to accomplish is vital! Knowing where you want to end up will determine which aim or aims you will stress.

REAL PLACES, REAL TIME
Putting Historical Events in the Correct Place and Time

by Ronald G. Davis

Studying history demands both a geographical and a chronological context. Such elements are part of what distinguishes truth from fantasy. Real events happen at real places. Real people experience real events. And real events always happen in relationship to other real events. There is no "Once upon a time," no "East of the sun and west of the moon," and no "In a far, far kingdom where it was always summer."

The Bible records real history. Real people. Real events. Real places. Real time. Its history is orderly and progressive. People are born, live, and die. Generation follows generation. A study in the book of Genesis offers an excellent opportunity to focus on the real history nature of the Bible. It traces the course of human history from two in a garden to a nation in Egypt. Generations and centuries pass, yet God is as present with Joseph at the end of Genesis as he is with Adam at the beginning. His expectations for the gardener are the same as they are for the governor. And both Adam and Joseph are free to make their own history—for good or for evil.

Wise teachers of history insist that their students know both the chronology and the geography of the material at hand. Such information is essential, for the temporal and spatial elements confirm the reality of significant people and the events of which they are a part.

A study of the life of Abraham—the man with whom God established his covenant and through whom he intended to bless "all peoples on earth" (Genesis 12:3)—should be a frequent experience. Abraham is such an important character that Paul and James, as well as the writer of Hebrews, base powerful arguments on his experiences. Thus the study of his life should be common, but it should never be ordinary.

Teaching Places

The geography of Abraham's life is the geography of the Old Testament. The territory that includes Ur to Egypt, that stretches from the area of the Tigris and Euphrates Rivers to the land of the Nile River, became "center stage" for the unfolding of God's redemptive plan, culminating in the birth of his Son in an obscure but real Judean town. Familiarity with this geographical framework is critical to a thorough understanding of God's revelation and activity.

A map of Abraham's world on display throughout your study of Abraham's life will be an important part of your teaching strategy. And with maps, the general instructional principle is "the bigger, the better." Even though the use of commercial maps can be beneficial, involving class members in the preparation and use of maps can be even more profitable. Look at the large open spaces available in your classroom: walls, tabletops, the floor, a bulletin board. Consider transferring a small outline of the land and water sites mentioned above to one or more of these spaces. If your congregation has an overhead projector, you can use an outline you have traced onto plastic to project a larger outline on the wall or on a large bulletin board. Masking tape (colored, if available) can be twisted to follow basic land lines. Or, for a bulletin board, yarn can be stapled into land shapes.

The traditional grid method of transferring an image can be used on any available surface. The original small map is ruled into squares (one-inch squares should work). Then the large surface is also lined into much larger squares in some fashion. Walls can be ruled with narrow masking tape; tabletops can be ruled with washable markers (or erasable pencil lines); in some cases, floors have the natural grid of square floor tiles. Make the squares on the larger surface proportionately larger and then put in the lines designating the land areas square by square. Most maps highlighting Abraham's geography that are found in the back of a Bible will be about 4" by 8" for the area covered. Thus, if your wall has a 4' by 8' area, the squares can be one-foot squares, and the resulting map will be 144 times the size of the original!

However you decide to do this project, recruit two or three class members to help you with the work. Recruit one or two others to letter appropriately sized place-name cards. During the class session in which a specific place is introduced, have someone stick the proper name on the map. Whatever map(s) you prepare, be certain to give the students a scale of miles: "one inch equals ____ miles." This will give students an appreciation of the rigors of Abraham's travels.

Cartographic precision is not your goal in this project, so don't be too concerned with details. General knowledge of bodies of water, cities, and the relationships of different areas to one another is what matters most. Abraham lived and moved in real places; your students need the ever-present reminder of what and where those real places were and are.

Teaching Time

Young children have often been taught the "big hand, little hand" method of telling time. (Today's students are probably more familiar with digital timepieces.) Genesis is a history of real people and real events. Those who study it need to be able to "tell time"—to know beginnings from middles and middles from ends. Chronology gives evidence of validity and believability. At every point during a study from Genesis you, as a teacher, will want to emphasize the sequence of people and events. Once a student of the Bible learns to "tell time," he or she is much closer to grasping the sequence of events within God's master plan.

Early in the study you may find it helpful to give your students a list of the primary people of Genesis arranged in alphabetical order and ask them to put the names in chronological order. (You might use Abraham, Adam, Enoch, Eve, Hagar, Isaac, Ishmael, Jacob, Joseph, Lot, Methuselah, Noah, Rebekah, Sarah, and Terah.) One way of doing this would be to give each student a letter-sized sheet of paper divided into 15 boxes, with one name in each box. Ask your class to tear the names apart and stack them up from earliest to latest. When you announce the correct order, each person can check his or her work.

With some lessons, you may choose to condense the main story to six to ten key events written as sentences on strips of paper. Ask your class to place these in the correct sequence. For example, a lesson that surveys the four chapters given to Noah and the flood (Genesis 6–9) includes several details. Consider presenting the following ten sentences randomly to your class and asking the students to put them in correct order: (1) God tells Noah to build an ark. (2) Representative animals are gathered. (3) Rain falls for forty days and nights. (4) The flood covers the earth for one hundred fifty days. (5) The ark comes to rest on Ararat. (6) A raven is sent from the ark. (7) A dove is sent out twice. (8) Noah's family comes out of the ark. (9) Noah sacrifices to the Lord. (10) God provides the rainbow as a sign.

Joseph's Time

When you launch a study of the life of Joseph (Genesis 37–50), use the following collection of objects to help give an overview of his life: a piece of bright plaid cloth, twenty pieces of silver (dimes), a torn robe or shirt, two sets of seven calendars, handcuffs or chains, a sack of flour, a silver cup, and a small doll wrapped in gauze (like a mummy). Display the objects randomly to your class, and ask them to decide in what order to put the items to represent Joseph's life.

Here are the answers: *cloth*=Joseph's coat of many colors; *twenty dimes*=the price of Joseph's slavery; *robe*=Potiphar's wife's act of lust; *chains*=imprisonment; *sets of calendars*=sets of seven years in Pharaoh's dream; *flour*=the plenty in Egypt; *cup*=Benjamin's sack of grain and silver; *doll*=embalmed Joseph.

Choose more or other objects if you think they will be more effective in telling the story.

Most students learn specific events best when they have a historic framework or overview. Most students learn history better when they can picture the geography of the area where the history takes place. Do all you can during your study of real history to aid your students in their understanding of the significant events and places of Genesis.

RECEIVING GOD'S CALL

He Can't Be Put on Hold

by Ronald G. Davis

God's call has come to men and women in a variety of ways, from the direct address to Adam and Eve in the garden to the indirect call of the written Word. What ultimately matters regarding his call is our response. All must decide: run and hide as Adam and Eve tried, or pack up and follow as the seaside fishermen did.

Calling in the Twenty-first Century

One marvel of the twenty-first century is the discovery of God's secrets of creation. From magnetic digital patterns to electrons "floating" through the air, humanity has discovered and established dominion over the science God put into place at creation. Many calls now come through wireless phones and cyberspace e-mails.

As one strategy for helping learners attend to and internalize the lessons, develop a pattern of sending an e-mail or text messaging blast of a weekly truth as a preview of the following Sunday's study. Consider the following weekly messages (taken from a past study of divine calls in the Gospels):

- "Simeon and Anna were called to wait. Could you do it?"
- "The first disciples were called to leave successful vocations. Could you do it?"
- "Matthew was called to leave a position of privilege and prosperity. Could you do it?"
- "Twelve were called to fill specific servant ministries. Could you do it?"
- "All disciples are called to change their central focus: from self to Christ. Can you do it?"
- "James and John were called to leave behind their ideas of self-aggrandizement for submission and service. Could you do it?"
- "Nicodemus was called to admit his own inadequate knowledge and understanding. Could you do it?"
- "The Samaritan woman at the well was called to face and admit her sins. Could you do it?"

Telephone Calls from Heaven

Stand-up comedians have used the concept of "one-sided" telephone calls with great success. To contemporize God's call to the people in Scripture, consider developing a "script" for one or more such lessons. You may have a class member who would delight in such an opportunity. Here are two examples, the call of Abram and the call of Matthew:

"Hello, this is Abram. Who is this calling? [pause] Yahweh? [pause] You want me to go where? [pause] Oh, you'll show me when I need to know. [pause] Leave my people behind? Uh huh. [pause] Great nation? Uh huh. [pause] Great name? Oh, sure. [pause] Great blessing? But Lord, I feel blessed right here. [pause] All the families of the earth? How many is that, Lord? [pause] I wouldn't believe it? [pause] Trust you? Uh huh. Can I take anyone with me, Lord? [pause] Sarai, good! [pause] My nephew? Okay. [pause] Canaan? Where's Canaan? [pause] Oh, okay, Lord. I'll see. Uh huh" [click].

"Matthew, CTC—Certified Tax Collector—How may I help you? [pause] Well, I'm kind of busy today, Jesus. [pause] This is my opportunity? Today? This is a pretty successful business I've got here, Lord. [pause] Well, yes, it does have its downside—hatred, resentment, and all that. [pause] Uh huh. That's true, Lord. Your kingdom is more important than Rome's. [pause] Right now, Lord? Can we discuss this over dinner? I'll invite a few friends. [pause] Follow first, feast later? [pause] Let me shut down my office and hand in my commission, Lord. See you at my house. [hangs up] What have I done?"

Such a monologue could be an effective attention-directing activity to begin a class. Be sure to have a desk phone available as a prop. And at the end of the "call," be certain to discuss how accurately or inaccurately each portrays the biblical occasion (for example, the biblical account reveals no hesitancy on the part of Matthew to follow).

Calls Against Lifetime Longings

Have your class develop an acrostic for the phrase, "Call from God." Put the letters of these words vertically down a sheet that you can post or copy and distribute. Ask the class to suggest single words that begin with each of the letters that also characterize the call of God. It will be best if no two are relatively synonymous. Here are possibilities (but note that there are possible synonymous terms included): *challenging, cryptic, clear, abrupt, answerable, life-changing, liberating, frequent, far-reaching, repeated, revolutionary, open-handed, open-ended, mysterious, majestic, magnetic, gracious, gifted, oral, demanding.*

When you are ready to move from text study to application, ask your class to look at their list of characteristics as a checklist for the person(s) and the call(s) being studied. Go entry to entry. For example, for a lesson on the call of Abram, if the word for C were *cryptic*, the question would be, "In what sense, if any, did God's call to Abram carry any sense of puzzlement?"

If the word for G was *gifted*, the question could be, "In what way(s) did God enable ("gift") Abram to answer his call, as the difficulties arose?" Obviously, God left many of Abram's questions initially unanswered, but he supplied the wisdom and the means to meet any challenge to his obedience. Each week it is a simple matter of replacing the name to the person under consideration.

For the visually-oriented class, you might display images to suggest something about the call of the character that highlights your study. *For Abram*, a picture of a comfortable home, to represent his call from home and family; *for David*, a newspaper front page headlining corruption in high places, to represent a call to moral integrity; *for Joseph*, a daily planner, to represent God's call to change one's immediate and long-term plans; *for Simeon and Anna*, a calendar, to represent their long wait for God's revelation; *for the first disciples*, a classified ads page for jobs wanted, to represent a call from one job to another; *for Matthew*, play money, to represent his call from a lucrative job; *for the Twelve*, a picture of mountain backpackers with heavy loads, to represent the opposite of the Twelve's accoutrements; *for all disciples*, a decorative cross, to represent the ultimate call for self-sacrifice. At some point in the lesson, stop to ask whether someone can identify the relationship of the image to the study of the day.

We want every learner to know that God's call continues to this day and to every person. This is a call to the blessings of a relationship with him in his Son.

SOMETHING MORE

Imagery and Incompletions

by Ronald G. Davis

Teachers and learners alike have much to anticipate in the study of God's Word. The most important "teacher tip" for any teacher may be: "Get excited, and show it!" That's always true, but it seems even more on point when dealing with a study of the resurrection or the return of Christ. What could be more exciting?

As usual, the teaching ideas need to reflect in some way the basic content. Sometimes you can reflect that content in very tangible ways. Simple objects can take on deep, emotional significance as life is lived, and waiting for completion and fulfillment creates excitement when the anticipated outcome is good.

Special Things

Through the Bible revelation, God uses simple things as "thought provokers" for his people. Imagine Noah and his sons, after the flood, seeing a rainbow without recalling the stormy days afloat on a covered, dead world and without rejoicing in God's grand promise (see Genesis 9:12-17). Imagine Peter, at the end of his life, seeing (or hearing) a rooster without remembering his dark and ugly sin of denying he knew Jesus (see Matthew 26:33-35, 69-75). Every dawn would spur Peter to say, "Never again, Lord."

Consider the significant objects in the following texts from the final week leading to the death and resurrection of Christ:

Matthew 26:1-25—A container of rich anointing perfume becomes a memorial to the woman who poured it out on Jesus' head; thirty silver coins becomes a sign of infamy forever. You can offer attenders a "squirt" of (fragrance-free—for the hypersensitive) hand lotion as they arrive, or give each one a shiny dime as he or she leaves. Either offers a relational reminder for this week's study. The lotion given as members arrive and the coin given as they leave will represent the correct sequence of the events.

Luke 22:1-23—The simplest elements of the Passover meal take on the most profound meaning granted to any element of God's creation: the unleavened bread is Christ's body of death; the pure juice of the vine is Jesus' blood poured out at Calvary for sins. Simply having a cup or tray of juice and a plate of bread present as learners arrive will immediately foreshadow the study.

Matthew 26:36-50—A sign of deepest love (a kiss) becomes a stigma of despicable treachery. Handing out a chocolate kiss (or if your class would appreciate the symbolism, a pair of candy wax lips) to each member would be a useful reminder of lesson truths.

Mark 14:53—15:15—Having all the accoutrements of judicial power does not ensure justice will be done. Few things represent the courtroom better than a judicial gavel. The sound of wood on wood has the sound of finality and authority. A judge's robe, if one can be obtained, may carry the symbolism as well.

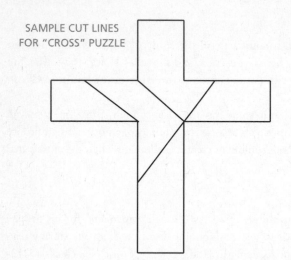

SAMPLE CUT LINES FOR "CROSS" PUZZLE

John 19:16-37—The cruel and unusual Roman execution technique of crucifixion yields an image worn with pride and honor by many Christians. For each learner have an envelope containing the pieces of a tangram-like puzzle made from a cut-out cross that has been further cut into three to five pieces (see sample at the left). Ask the group to assemble their pieces into a recognizable shape. Read 1 Corinthians 1:23, "We preach Christ crucified: a stumbling block to Jews and foolishness to Gentiles." Note that to many the cross is a puzzle, but to God it is both power and wisdom.

Matthew 28—Something empty (Jesus' tomb) fills the world for all time with endless hope. For each class member have a small, unadorned empty box. (If necessary, visit a packaging, shipping store where small [jewelry-sized] boxes can be bought inexpensively.) Put one on each seat before students arrive. Curiosity will drive many to open their boxes, discovering that they are empty. When some moan or joke about disappointment, note that, "Some empty things terminate hope; one empty thing gives hope!"

God is the Master of the symbolic. From the mark on Cain (Genesis 4:15) to the beautiful stones of the wall of the new Jerusalem (Revelation 21:10, 19, 20), God provides the imagery that catches the eye and fills the mind. The wise teacher will attempt to do the same.

Expecting Completion

A predictably successful way to stimulate initial thinking as learners arrive for class is simply to display a completion statement. Few can read a partial, incomplete statement without mentally finishing it.

Consider the following statements, based on the following texts:

1 Thessalonians 1—One Christian or church that brings a smile to my face is . . .

1 Thessalonians 4, 5— One of my Christian friends (or family) who has died and whom I am looking forward to seeing in Heaven is . . .

2 Thessalonians 2—Reflecting the glory of God is most difficult for me when . . .

Revelation 5—My favorite hymn/song of worship of Christ is . . .

Revelation 7—I have the most difficulty living a holy life when . . .

Revelation 14—Believing in Hell motivates me to . . .

Revelation 21—The kinds of people I see going to Hell are . . .

If your class has available a marker board or chalkboard, displaying "pieces" of words is sure to get a learner response. Writing key words from a lesson text and then erasing top halves or bottom halves or simply "swirling" an eraser through the words will have the viewers "filling in the blanks." (Be certain not to erase too much.) Consider some of the following words for the same lesson texts as above:

1 Thessalonians 1—thankful, prayers, hope, work.

1 Thessalonians 4, 5—wrath, salvation, ignorant, trump.

2 Thessalonians 2—glory, sanctification, traditions, evil.

Revelation 5—Lamb, worthy, book, seals.

Revelation 7—angel, multitude, Shepherd, tears.

Revelation 14—Babylon, judgment, voice, beast.

Revelation 21—new, his, Jerusalem, no.

What's Missing?

A similar effect can be achieved with a "What's Missing?" activity. This can be accomplished in a verbal activity in which statements are correct, and yet there is a key word or words missing. The challenge for the learner is to supply a missing word or words that maintain the truth of the statement in keeping with the context. Present the statements and say, "Each of these sentences is true. What word or words can be added to each that keep them true? What word or words will reflect today's lesson text?"

For example, for 1 Thessalonians 1, one could give the following statements (offered here with possible missing word in brackets): "Before Paul preached to the Thessalonians, they were [idol] worshipers" (1:9); or "Paul told the Thessalonians he was remembering their work [of faith] and labor [of love] and endurance [of hope]" (1:3).

For 1 Thessalonians 4, you could use the following statements: "When the Lord returns from Heaven, the dead [in Christ] will rise first" (4:16); or "Christians who are alive on the earth when the Lord comes will meet him [in the air]" (4:17).

Jigsaw Puzzles

Consider writing, in large print from edge to edge, a key verse from a lesson or a key truth on a piece of poster board. Cut the poster into twelve to sixteen approximately equal pieces in a jigsaw puzzle form. Hand out the pieces randomly as members arrive. At the appropriate point in your time of study, invite those who hold pieces to come to the front and stick their pieces on the wall or board (masking tape or Plasti-Tak should work) and arrange them correctly as they do. If you have an artistic class member, you might ask her or him to draw a relevant image on poster board and do the same as with the verses/ideas.

THE TEACHER'S DILEMMA:

"What's Next?"

Every few weeks, Sunday school classes must begin a new study. The question, "What should we study next?" makes us cringe because it comes up so often! Frequently, the study will be that of the teacher's own choice, and the focus may be limited to one of a half dozen favorite themes. Some classes decide by taking a vote, and the result is a curriculum with little structure and no plan for systematic Bible study.

Many teachers have discovered that the best solution to this problem lies in using a teaching commentary that offers International Sunday School Lessons (ISSL) from the Uniform Lesson Series. But how do you go about choosing a good teaching commentary? Five key factors may help you decide.

High View

Above all, a good teaching commentary must display a high view of Scripture. Such a view recognizes that the Bible is the Word of God for all generations. Its writers and editors are committed to that truth; it's the reason they do what they do. See Psalm 119:105; 2 Timothy 3:16, 17.

Comprehensive Coverage

From the first point naturally flows the second: the commentary should offer comprehensive Bible coverage. The Bible in its entirety is God's Word, so a good teaching commentary will present lessons that balance Old and New Testament studies. The best teaching commentaries that are based on the ISSL format do just that. Within a brief cycle of years, adults gain a good overview of the message of the Bible. The cycles that follow do not simply repeat the previous ones but shift to different passages. The treatment is fresh each time.

Relevant to Culture

Cultural relevance concerns the ability of the lesson to connect people in the here-and-now with the eternal, inspired truth of Scripture. The lessons in some commentaries stop when the text has been explored and the students informed of what the text meant in its original context. Better commentaries help the students to apply the principles to today's culture. This way, students do not leave the classroom wondering, "So what?"

Effective Communication

Closely related to cultural relevance is the ability of the lesson commentary to communicate effectively. The Bible is an ancient book, written in ancient languages. The translation may contain words or phrases that, even in English, sound strange to modern ears. These phrases should be explained or illustrated.

Unfortunately, some teaching commentaries make the mistake of trying to communicate too academically in such explanations. The mere fact that the students are adults and can understand complicated text does not mean they want to communicate at that level. Instead, many prefer to communicate through story. The better teaching commentaries use verbal illustrations to help reach these learners. That fact leads to the fifth key.

Variety of Methods

A good teaching commentary takes into account a variety of teaching methods and learning styles. Some commentaries provide little more than lecture material because that is the easiest kind of material to provide. But while lecture has its place—face it, adults who attend church are used to it—it is not always the best method. Adults like to discuss issues. Better teaching commentaries provide opportunities for them to answer the question, "What do you think?"

On the other hand some adults are more kinetic in their learning style. They love learning activities: crossword puzzles, word search exercises, journaling, drama, music, creative writing, etc. The better teaching commentaries provide these in addition to maps, charts, and Bible art as visual aids. Some commentaries are now available in digital form, making such resources as PowerPoint slides readily available. Pick up a good lesson commentary, and you'll never have to wonder, "What's next?" again.

Teaching for Transformed Lives

Our Privilege

by Eleanor A. Daniel

Teaching God's Word is a special privilege. But teaching God's Word to transform lives is more than a privilege—it is both work and a craft.

Effective teaching is always more than merely presenting a body of information, providing interpretation of the material, and suggesting a bit of an application. It also demands that the teacher "read" the learners and the needs, interests, and concerns they bring to the learning situation. It is this reality that always makes me muse longest as I prepare to teach.

Begin with a Central Truth

If you plan to teach the Word of God to transform lives, you must do the careful work of understanding the text and figuring out how it intersects with the lives of contemporary learners. It is by using your study of the text and your knowledge of your learners that you put together what I call the central truth for the lesson.

The central truth is a simple declarative sentence that provides the focus for the lesson and your preparation of it. It frequently combines Scripture content and student response. It is the thread that holds the lesson together. It is what you want the learners to remember even if they should forget all the details. It helps you decide how to approach the lesson, how many details to include, and what can wait until another teaching of the text.

The central truth of a passage usually is not hard to find. Here are some possibilities for a series of texts from Isaiah:

- *Isaiah 42:1-9:* God's servant came to deliver hope, justice, and righteousness to all people, even, perhaps especially, the disenfranchised among us.
- *Isaiah 49:5, 6; 50:4-11:* God's servant came to deliver salvation to all people, whatever their ethnic or personal background.
- *Isaiah 53:1-3:* God's suffering servant meets our deepest need: personal salvation.
- *Isaiah 61:1, 2:* Our response to the Lord's servant should be one of joyful praise and proclamation.

For a series of lessons on leadership from 1 Timothy, consider the following possibilities as central truths.

- *1 Timothy 1:12-20:* The effective leader is the one who has been transformed by Christ.
- *1 Timothy 2:1-8:* Effective leaders are characterized by a distinctively Christlike lifestyle that is marked by prayer.
- *1 Timothy 3:1-15:* Effective Christian elders model a life of piety and service for Christ.
- *1 Timothy 4:* Effective Christian leaders give close attention to biblical teaching.
- *1 Timothy 5:1-8, 17-25:* Effective Christian leaders and followers are marked by behavior that puts the needs of others first.

Another series from the Pastoral Epistles can provide a helpful study of the interaction between faithful leaders and their followers. Consider the following texts and central truths:

- *2 Timothy 1:3-14:* Effective Christian leaders and followers are called to influence others.
- *2 Timothy 2:14-26:* Effective Christian leaders and followers seek God's approval.
- *2 Timothy 3:10–4:8:* Effective Christian leaders and followers faithfully perform their duties, despite the circumstances.
- *Titus 2:* All Christians are responsible to see that the Word of God is taught to those of all ages.

Next, Think About Presentation

When your course is set by a clear central truth, you are ready to think about how you will present the material. Bible lessons designed to transform lives have four building blocks that, when taken altogether, lead the student to the Word of God and from there to life.

Building Block #1: Approach. How will you gain the learners' attention? To begin by announcing the Scripture reference is not likely to engage adults. Instead, you could open with a good illustration and ask how it applies. Another approach is to have the learners interact with a concept relevant to the lesson. Still another option is to make a statement related to the lesson and ask students to agree or disagree.

Starting the lesson with a question is another tried-and-true method of gaining attention. You could take your central truth and modify it to be this question. Or you may wish to consider the following sample questions for the same three series of lessons suggested above.

- *Isaiah 42:1-9:* What do people hope for today? Why?
- *Isaiah 49:5, 6; 50:4-11:* What is salvation? What do people want to be saved from? What do they want to be saved to?
- *Isaiah 53:1-3:* What are some words related to salvation?
- *Isaiah 61:1, 2:* What do you do when you learn good news?
- *1 Timothy 1:12-20:* What qualities do leaders need most to be effective in the church?
- *1 Timothy 2:1-8:* Is it possible for a leader who does not demonstrate fully the qualities of Christ to lead effectively? Why, or why not?

- *1 Timothy 3:1-15:* If you were to craft a statement of what an elder in our church should be like, how would you illustrate this list for modern culture?
- *1 Timothy 4:* What does it mean to say that our church provides biblical teaching?
- *1 Timothy 5:1-8, 17-25:* How is it possible for Christian leaders to put the needs of others first and still attend to their own needs?
- *2 Timothy 1:3-14:* How have others influenced you?
- *2 Timothy 2:14-26:* As you were growing up, whose approval did you seek most of all? Why? How has that changed—or stayed the same—since childhood and adolescence?
- *2 Timothy 3:10–4:8:* What are some words that you associate with the concept of "duty"?
- *Titus 2:* What do each of the age groups of preschool, elementary school, youth, and adults in our church need to learn? Who should teach them?

These are just possibilities—there are many more! You can also develop this building block for the class as a whole or for small groups. Your decision here will depend on the nature of your class and the type of approach you decide on from week to week.

Remember that your goal is to engage your students from the very outset. This building block could be your most important, so don't bypass it! When you engage learners' attention at the very beginning, they are far more likely to remain involved as you move to the more complex material. When learners hear their own voices early in the session, they are much more likely to continue participating.

Building Block #2: Bible Study. The second building block is a study of the Scripture itself. What does it say? What questions does it answer? What questions does it raise? How should it be interpreted?

You have many tools at your disposal. Each lesson demands some means of engaging learners in the lesson. Discussion questions, for instance, should be designed to elicit productive interaction. You need not resort to lecture for every lesson; try a variety of learning activities that involve more of the learners' senses than just hearing.

If you are serious about wanting your learners to participate in discussion, encourage it from the beginning and throughout. People rarely participate in discussions that are tacked on as an afterthought following a lengthy lecture.

Building Block #3: Application. The proof of the lesson is in how learners are challenged to weave the teaching of the Bible text into their lives. Many will do it on their own, but don't assume that everyone will. Take some time to raise questions, suggest applications, and think through how Bible lessons learned can transform lives. Whatever you do, don't skip the application!

Building Block #4: Conclusion. When you get to the end of the text and application, don't just stop. Take some time to summarize what you have discovered. Tell a story that elicits response. Challenge the learners. Pray with the class members to encourage them in their Christian journey.

The conclusion does not have to be long—in fact, it probably should not be. It need not be if you have followed the procedure suggested thus far. Your conclusion can be as short as verbalizing the central truth and asking the class to repeat it with you. The conclusion may be delivered in the form of a story or illustration that serves as a memorable summary or wrap-up.

After Class

Take a few minutes after you have finished teaching to reflect on how things went. Which activities did the learners respond to well? What needs to be modified? Which explanations did they "get"? Which ones should you have thought through more carefully? Self-reflection may be one of the best tools that you have for consistently improving your teaching.

One last word: Relax and enjoy your teaching experience. If you have prepared well, you will have far more successes than failures. And even a bad day isn't the end. Usually your class is forgiving. And it is amazing what we learn from a bad day now and then!

TEACHING THE BORED

Part 1 in a Series of Problem Student Tips

by Brent L. Amato

We are called by God to teach his people (2 Timothy 2:2, 24). Each student in your class is precious in his sight, each a gift from him. Your students are the reason for and the object of your teaching ministry. No students, no need for a teacher!

"But you don't know some of my students!" you might say. Admit it: in a weaker moment, haven't you contemplated how much easier, exciting, and rewarding teaching would be if you could select your own students? Haven't you wished from time to time that certain students wouldn't show up?

But "problem students" come with the teaching turf. In our mind's eye, we can almost see each problem student marching into our classroom with a big sign hanging around his or her neck proclaiming one of four identities: *the bored, the barrier, the boss,* and *the bomber.* We may wish they wouldn't come, but they must be taught!

Four Types, One Imperative

Pray for these students. Pray for them by name. Intercessory prayer is commanded frequently in the New Testament (Colossians 4:3; 1 Thessalonians 5:25; Hebrews 13:18). What could happen if you started praying daily this week for them?

Pray for these students the same thing you should pray for all your students: that the Word of God you teach will accomplish what God desires in them (Isaiah 55:11) and pierce them to the depths of their soul and spirit (Hebrews 4:12). But your prayers on behalf of these students should also be as specific as possible. Pray about the cause of their problem behavior. What is causing them to be bored? Why do they feel they need so much attention? What is causing their resistance? Pray that God will deal with the issues in their lives that are creating problems. And pray that you will be sensitive to their needs and respond appropriately.

God is in the business of redemption, and that includes students in Bible study classes. To accomplish the goal of redemption, he first must get the attention of his children! Intercessory prayer is vital for connecting these students with our awesome God, who is the antidote for all that cuts against your teaching.

One Focus, Three Strategies

For this chapter, we'll focus on *the bored* and deal with the other three in subsequent chapters. For whatever reason, you aren't connecting with the bored. It appears that they wish they were somewhere else. Although physically present, they are absent mentally, emotionally, and—most important—spiritually. Let's consider three ways to make progress with your bored students.

First, shift into a higher gear. Vary your teaching methods; this will keep you out of "teaching ruts" that can fuel boredom. Your bored student may have a learning style that is different from your teaching style. Deliberately force yourself to use more variety.

Bored students typically feel Sunday school is not for them. Perhaps they are there because their spouse insists on it. Or they bring their children and have "nothing better to do" during the Sunday school hour. Let your bored students know they do belong in your class. Make frequent eye contact with them. Give them special attention. Ask them questions. Ask them to do some research ("homework") in preparation for your next class. Show that you care for them and are not bored in teaching them.

Second, probe for passion. Take every opportunity to engage your bored students in conversation. Cultivate a relationship with them outside the classroom. In so doing, you may discover some of their passions, which you can build into your teaching as an antidote to their boredom.

Third, don't beat up either "the bored" or yourself. Once you have done what you can to improve your teaching and to engage the bored student, accept the fact that there will be some students in your class who would rather be somewhere else on a given day. The fact that some students are bored doesn't necessarily mean that you are a bad teacher. Realizing these facts will reduce the pressure to be "the perfect teacher" and reduce your frustration toward "the imperfect student." Keep teaching in spite of them.

I can't wait for my next class! I hope my bored students show up. What about you?

TEACHING THE BARRIER

Part 2 in a Series of Problem Student Tips

by Brent L. Amato

The previous chapter launched us on a consideration of four types of "problem students" who make their presence felt in the classroom: *the bored, the barrier, the boss, and the bomber.* We addressed the first of these four last time; now let's turn our attention to the second. We will consider the remaining two in the next two chapters.

Four Types, More Imperatives

The New Testament offers imperatives regarding how Christians are to relate to each other. We mentioned the imperative of intercessory prayer above. But there are other imperatives to consider as well.

Many imperatives are found in the New Testament's "one another" passages. We are to love one another (John 13:34). We are to be devoted to one another and honor one another (Romans 12:10). We are to accept one another as Christ accepted us (Romans 15:7). If you take some time to scan through the "one another" passages, you'll see that this just scratches the surface!

These passages serve to remind us that good teaching involves much more than mastery of teaching techniques. To reach your students, you must have a Spirit-filled relationship with them. Such a relationship will have much more to do with your effectiveness as a teacher than the brilliance of your lesson plan and presentation.

The Master's teaching was always relational, and you can tailor the "one anothers" specifically to each student, no matter what category they fall in. The fact that the teacher communicates relationally with the students beyond the Sunday school hour is a powerful antidote for all that would otherwise hinder the effectiveness of your teaching.

One Strategy, Three Steps

Let's focus on *the barrier*. This student, unlike *the bored*, is engaged and sincerely has something to offer during class. Unfortunately, the barrier's contribution has nothing to do with your lesson!

You need a strategy for dealing with this situation that affirms both the barrier and the class while keeping the class on target.

Picture this: You're making good headway as you teach a lesson on devotional life from the Psalms. Suddenly, the barrier asks a question that deals with the end times! We call this kind of question a "rabbit trail"; if you start down that path, you'll be a long time trying to get to the end. It is a distraction from your lesson and should not be pursued.

How do we deal with such a barrier? Let's explore three steps to take in order to keep your class on task without doing harm to the person who is a barrier.

First, know your lesson plan and stick to it. Granted, there will always be legitimate "detours" or some need to be attended to. But detours should be the exception and not the rule. Lesson outlines help not only you but also the students in this regard. Use your lesson plan as a litmus test for the relevancy of the barrier's issues, comments, and questions. If the question is completely unrelated to the lesson's purpose, you will not entertain it.

Second, affirm both the barrier and the rest of the class when confronted with a rabbit trail. Rather than ignoring, rejecting, or challenging the barrier's comment or question, affirm the barrier by briefly acknowledging the importance of his or her point. But then graciously remind the barrier that while there is a time for everything (Ecclesiastes 3:1), the time for that topic is not now, but that you are available to discuss it after class. Affirm the class as a whole by quickly moving on and sticking with the lesson.

Third, address the barrier's point with him or her personally right after class or as soon as possible. It is your relationship with the barrier and not the detour or even your lesson that is paramount. Your positive action in this regard will speak volumes to your students. If you do not touch base after class with the student who has a question—either to answer the question or to arrange a time to discuss it—then you have done nothing but simply brush off that student. This is rude and will do harm to your relationship with that student and with the class.

As with the other three types, I hope my barrier students show up! May you rise to the challenge of teaching all your problem students effectively for the glory of God.

TEACHING THE BOSS

Part 3 in a Series of Problem Student Tips

by Brent L. Amato

By now you know that classroom challenges are sometimes presented by one of four types of "problem students": *the bored, the barrier, the boss, and the bomber.* As we address the third of these, remember that God loves every student in your classroom, and you've been called to be an equal opportunity teacher!

Four Types, Yet Another Imperative

Our previous installments highlighted two imperatives: intercessory prayer on behalf of your learners and relating to your learners in accordance with the New Testament "one another" passages. These still apply!

Another imperative is to "parent" your learners as Paul did his. Paul described Timothy as "my true son in the faith" (1 Timothy 1:2; see also 1 Corinthians 4:17 and 2 Timothy 1:2); Titus was Paul's "true son in our common faith" (Titus 1:4). Of course, Timothy and Titus were coworkers with Paul; he mentored them for special ministry. So you may think their relationship with Paul is not relevant to your relationship with your learners. But Paul could consider himself a "father" to large groups as well; consider 1 Corinthians 4:15, where Paul tells the Corinthians "in Christ Jesus I became your father through the gospel." How would your attitudes and actions toward your problem students be different if you viewed them as your spiritual children?

Parents know, of course, that there is a time to be confrontational with their children (compare 1 Corinthians 4:14-16; Galatians 3:1; 4:19, 20). But surely a gentle, nurturing mother or an encouraging, comforting father is the primary model for making the most progress with a child (1 Thessalonians 2:11, 12)!

All your learners need spiritual parenting. Paul's spiritual parenting of the Thessalonians is a touchstone for investing yourself in the lives of your learners: "Because we loved you so much, we were delighted to share with you not only the gospel of God but our lives as well" (1 Thessalonians 2:8). This gets to the core of the matter: your heart connected with the hearts of your learners.

One Focus, Three Strategies

Let's consider now *the boss* in your classroom. You can't miss him; he's the one who typically dominates your lesson, especially when you open it up for discussion. Can't you almost hear him thinking, "I've got so much to say and so little time"? Can't you see her grabbing center stage and holding on for dear life? The boss is lurking in every classroom, ready to stifle the learning process for everyone.

As with the other types of challenging students, there are certain strategies available for dealing with the boss. Let's consider three.

First, control the boss. As he or she expounds, take heart that everyone has to take a breath. When the boss does that, seize the moment by interrupting with a terminating affirmation by saying something like, "Interesting point!" Then exercise "benign neglect" by moving your eyes and body away from the boss to others in the classroom. Immediately direct your attention and/or call on someone else in a different section of the classroom. Hopefully the boss will get the message. If not, repeat the method as many times as necessary.

Second, connect with the boss. Spend time with the boss outside the classroom. Get with him or her one-on-one and utter those words this kind of student loves to hear: "Tell me more!" You will save precious class time, spare the other learners, develop your relationship with the boss, and even sharpen your listening skills. Such "overtime" will earn you the right to confront the boss lovingly about the issue. It will also help you mentor the boss into effective ministry. And that is the third strategy.

Third, channel the boss. Like directing water along a predetermined path, direct the boss into new areas of ministry. Find an appropriate forum for the boss. Be aware that the boss may be another effective teacher in the making. Perhaps this person deserves a teaching platform. Perhaps there is another class in need of a teacher, and this person could fill that role. Release your own class to the boss so that you can launch a new one. Perhaps the boss has potential but is not yet ready to teach alone. Try team-teaching with the boss or suggest another mentor who can help.

Never grow weary because of problem students! Just keep drawing on the grace and power of God to teach all who walk into your classroom.

TEACHING THE BOMBER

Part 4 in a Series of Problem Student Tips

by Brent L. Amato

Having read the previous three chapters, you know by now that *the bored, the barrier, the boss,* and *the bomber* are four types of problem students who present themselves in your classroom. This chapter will address the fourth and most dangerous of these.

The bomber enters your classroom looking for targets. He or she may take verbal aim at your lesson, the other learners, and/or you personally! For some reason, the bomber seems to have the proverbial "chip on his shoulder" that results in lashing out. Whether the bomber is simply misguided or intentionally malicious, failure to deal with the situation can mean the destruction of your class.

Jesus, the master teacher, had to deal with both kinds of bombers. Peter was one of the "misguided" kind on at least one occasion (see Matthew 16:21-23). Many Pharisees were of the "intentionally malicious" ilk (see Mark 12:13-17). Jesus didn't let the bombers' agendas succeed in his day, and neither can we in ours.

One More Imperative

Our previous chapters offered three imperatives for all four types of problem students: intercessory prayer, relating to these individuals in accordance with the New Testament's "one another" passages, and spiritual parenting. One additional imperative specifically applies to you, the teacher: *never give up.*

After an especially vexing class, haven't we all asked ourselves, "Why do I continue to teach? Why do I even bother?" We easily can picture the apostle Paul asking himself the same questions many times, especially after undergoing the physical bombings of whippings, beatings, and stoning (2 Corinthians 11:23-29). Paul continually found his teaching under bombardment by both misguided and malicious bombers (Galatians 2:11-14; 3:1-5). But Paul never gave up. "Let us not become weary in doing good, for at the proper time we will reap a harvest if we do not give up" (Galatians 6:9).

One Focus, Three Strategies

Your classroom may have nice lighting, comfortable chairs, and other fine accouterments, but it is also a battlefield. Satan's goal is to destroy, and he will fill your classroom with every kind of spiritual land mine, bullet, and bomb that he can. Thus we need some strategies to defeat his intentions.

First, prepare yourself with the realization that your teaching will be subject to spiritual attack. This just goes with the territory. If Jesus and Paul experienced bombers, why shouldn't you? Before you walk onto your classroom battlefield, make sure to "put on the full armor of God, so that you can take your stand against the devil's schemes" (Ephesians 6:11). Effective teachers are not only prepared with a lesson, but also clothed in spiritual armor.

Second, guard the truth and the class. There are doctrinal nonnegotiables, and you must be able to defend them from attack (2 Timothy 2:15). Seek to defuse the bomber quickly, calmly, and graciously (Proverbs 15:1). If at all possible, defer a confrontation until after class. In extreme cases, the protection of your flock may require that the bomber not be allowed to return to your class (Titus 3:10). If the situation is potentially at that point, then the elders need to be consulted about how to deal with the person. If he or she is bombing your class, then they are probably planting land mines in other areas of the church as well. Extreme discipline, beyond what you are in a position to administer, may be necessary. Our third strategy may help keep the situation from reaching that point.

Third, minister to the bomber outside the classroom. The root of the problem may be unresolved conflict, deep-seated emotional pain, a doctrinal agenda, unrepentant sin, or a personality issue directed toward you in particular. Finding out what's going on inside the bomber should be a priority, and this may require lots of time and tact. It may also require involving other people: leaders such as the elders, the minister, or a counselor in your church.

Remember that the goal is redemption and restoration (Galatians 6:1); the method for that is a blend of love and truth (Ephesians 4:15). A redeemed and restored bomber may be the best lesson you ever teach!

TESTING AS TOOL
Using Tests to Facilitate Learning

by James Riley Estep, Jr.

The word *test* may conjure up bad memories of a teacher strolling down a classroom aisle, slowly handing anxious students their midterm exams. With such a negative association, why would we consider using testing with our Bible lessons?

We certainly do not wish to inflict "test anxiety" on our learners! But with a bit of creativity, we can use testing as a tool of instruction.

"Before"

Testing can be used to introduce the Bible lesson. Testing at the outset of the lesson helps learners see gaps in their knowledge, showing them why they need the lesson. For example, Bible teachers often distribute a "Christmas Quiz" to start a lesson during that season. Typical questions on such a quiz include the following: "How many Magi were there?" (Answer: "The Bible doesn't say.") "What was the name of the innkeeper who opened his stable to Mary and Joseph?" (Answer: Again, the Bible makes no mention of an innkeeper or of a stable.) These questions expose the great amount of tradition and speculation that have become accepted as part of the Nativity story but are not in the Bible. This awareness can create an eagerness to fill in the gaps.

"During"

Testing also can be used in the middle of the Bible lesson as a way to measure students' understanding of the lesson as it progresses. Such a test can take many forms: true/false, multiple choice, matching, and listing are typical. But testing need not take the form of a written quiz. It also can be in the form of questions you pose verbally to the class as a whole. Most students won't even see this as a "test," but it accomplishes the same goals.

You should keep in mind, however, that there are different types of questions. Some deal with *knowledge* (recall of facts), others deal with *comprehension* (understanding how facts fit together), while others address *application* (what difference it should make in the student's life). Questions of knowledge and comprehension have "right" answers, while questions involving application tend to be open-ended. Application questions thus lend themselves more to discussion than to testing as we are using that term here. Each type of question has its place, and the distinctions among them should be recognized.

"After"

Testing at the end of the lesson can reveal whether your learning goals have been met. One common follow-up test is to ask students to summarize the lesson (or a series of lessons on a common theme). For example, you can ask learners to jot on index cards their responses to a certain question that an unbeliever might ask on the subject of the lesson or lessons at hand. Volunteers can share their answers as you create a joint, classroom response.

Some teachers use a pretest before the unit or quarter begins, then distribute the very same test questions at the end of the unit or quarter. This procedure alerts the student to what he or she should expect to learn in the weeks ahead, then provides a way to self-discover what the progress has been in that regard at the end.

Obstacles

Some teachers are not comfortable with using testing as a teaching method. The first obstacle, therefore, is the teacher's own willingness to try something new! Try using testing only periodically at first. This will help you develop a feel for what works best with your class.

A second obstacle involves the students. Let's face it: adults do not like to "be wrong" in front of other adults! When using written tests, you can minimize anxiety and fear of embarrassment at "being wrong" by informing your learners that (1) they are going to score the quizzes themselves and (2) you, the teacher, are not going to collect the completed quizzes. You can minimize learners' anxiety with verbalized test questions by posing the questions to the class as a whole and then allowing volunteers to respond.

Testing can increase your effectiveness as a teacher. Don't allow your own hesitation or that of your students to rob you of this valuable tool.

"THAT YOU MAY BELIEVE"

Making Your Case in the Classroom

by Ronald G. Davis

As a writer, the apostle John follows a time-honored strategy: a clear-cut theme and purpose, supported with carefully chosen example after example. His theme? "Jesus is the Christ, the Son of God!" His purpose? To convince all of that one grand truth, so that all may receive life in him. This treatise, from John's pen and by the power of the Spirit, is a thorough and convincing argument of his central thesis. Beginning with a resounding affirmation of Jesus' preexistence and full Godness, John furnishes testimony upon testimony, miracle upon miracle, insight upon insight.

Such a writer is overwhelmed by the vastness of his material—so much so that he is led to conclude, "If I had written it all down, I suppose the whole world would not have room for the books!" And he wants his readers to know that he has carefully chosen, from a wealth of possibilities, a selective but more than adequate sampling to prove his point: Jesus is the Christ, the Son of God!

The teacher who leads in a study of the Gospel of John must share John's purpose and strategy: to convince, to convince with evidence, and to convince with overwhelming evidence. Discussion and debate can serve as the heart of the teacher's instructional plan. Students should be unequivocal in affirming: "Jesus is the Christ, the Son of God!" They should be more fully "prepared to give an answer to everyone who asks . . . to give the reason for the hope" they possess in Jesus "with gentleness and respect" (1 Peter 3:15).

Determining who a person is can be achieved by posing three questions: (1) What do others say about him? (2) What does he say about himself? and (3) What do his deeds say about him? John uses all three of these lines of testimony in his Gospel. Consider how you as a teacher can "argue your case" that Jesus is the Christ, the Son of God.

What Others Say

John the Baptist's testimony to who Jesus is immediately follows the apostle John's grand opening statement declaring Jesus to be the Word, who "became flesh and made his dwelling among us" (John 1:14). In a court of law, a witness's testimony is both heard and evaluated. For any lesson dealing with someone's personal testimony, the following learning activity could be used effectively.

Recruit three class members to play these "courtroom" roles: prosecutor, defense attorney, and John the Baptist (or the "witness" in the specific text chosen). The prosecutor is playing the role of one of the priests and Levites from Jerusalem who came to interrogate John (John 1:19). The defense attorney is speaking on behalf of God. Establish a courtroom scene before your class, and tell the class members that they are to serve as the jury.

If your "actors" are willing and able, let them write their own questions. But if not, prepare and assign a few. For example, for the prosecutor: "John, tell this court exactly who you are." "Who do you claim Jesus to be?" "Don't you have some personal doubts about who he is?" "Who gave you authority to preach?" "Where did you get your training—if any—in the law and its interpretation?" "Why should we believe your word above that of those specially trained in religious matters?" "John, wouldn't you characterize your lifestyle as just a bit . . . well . . . eccentric?" "Don't you claim to hear voices—such as that of God—on a regular basis?"

For the defense attorney, suggest such questions as these: "How would you characterize your parents?" "Tell the court about the strange nature of your birth, John." "What was your father told about you before your conception?" "Are some still alive who can testify of seeing your awestruck and mute father when he came out of the temple? What of those who were present when his voice returned?" "Are you doing all of this preaching simply to draw attention and fame to yourself?" Your "John" may want to examine these references to prepare himself: Luke 1:5-23, 57-80; Matthew 3:1-17; Mark 1:1-11; Luke 3:1-22; John 1:19-27; 3:25-30.

After the question and answer period, charge the "jury" to decide whether John the Baptist is a credible witness. Ask them to explain why they accept his testimony.

You may choose to study one of the other "personal testimony" lessons in a similar manner. Imagine how the Samaritan woman could impress a courtroom! Picture Nicodemus or Thomas on the stand! The witnesses speak. Let them speak!

What He Says of Himself

One is always justified—even compelled—to determine who a person is by examining what he says of himself or what he claims himself to be. Jesus' claims are astounding; if they are true, they cannot be ignored!

When teaching on the text where Jesus claims to be "the bread of life" (John 6:35), you will have a good opportunity with your students to analyze Jesus' claims and decide why believing in him is both reasonable and essential.

Divide your class into groups of four or five and give each group the following list of texts from John. In each, Jesus affirms who he is: 4:25, 26; 6:35, 38; 8:58; 10:9, 30; 11:25, 26;

14:6, 9; 17:5. Ask each group to survey the texts, list the affirmations, and then arrange them in order of magnitude or significance. Assure students that this is not intended to lessen any of the truths; it is simply a way to consider the impact of each claim. Have the groups share and defend their choices.

Such a procedure could also be used with John 15, where Jesus characterizes himself as "the true vine," or John 4, where he avows, "Whoever drinks the water I give them will never thirst. . . [It] will become in them a spring of water welling up to eternal life" (John 4:14).

Some skeptics, wanting to discredit Jesus at every opportunity, have said Jesus never claimed to be deity. Help your class members to see the above passages from John as obvious and irrefutable evidence to the contrary. Jesus clearly claimed to be fully God. Are those who question this willing to give the evidence a fair hearing?

What His Deeds Say

A tree is known by its fruit. Seeing what fruit issues from a life is the best confirmation of the character and quality of that life. Words without deeds are inadequate. Thus, to say finally and conclusively that Jesus is the Christ, the Son of the living God, necessitates an examination of his deeds. Do his deeds reveal divine character? Do his deeds demonstrate divine power?

The Gospel of John offers proof to substantiate both answers in the affirmative. Jesus does personify the character and the power of God. Full insight into new acquaintances such as Nicodemus and the Samaritan woman reveal his omniscience. Feeding a multitude with a small amount of food demonstrates his power to supersede the "laws of nature." Jesus can do this because he is God—he wrote the "laws"!

Lessons on the crucifixion and resurrection of Jesus always call for special effort. Jesus is Savior, giving his life on the cross to redeem mankind in love and grace; and Jesus is Lord, conquering death by his resurrection. No greater truths will ever be presented! When teaching such a lesson, consider handing each class member an index card with the label *believer* or *doubter* written on it as he or she enters. Use equal numbers of *believer* and *doubter* cards. At some point in the lesson, have the class form pairs, with a believer and a doubter in each pair. The believer should ask the doubter, "How could you doubt . . . ?" and the doubter should ask the believer, "How could you believe . . . ?" Follow the word *doubt* or *believe* with some summary statement of the lesson text, a report by one of the witnesses, or some other alleged fact in the "case." Point out that some of the early followers of Jesus accepted news of his resurrection with ease and confidence (for example, Mary Magdalene in John 20:18), while others were much more resistant (the classic example is Thomas in John 20:24, 25). As your students identify before the class what they believe are the most cogent reasons for each position, ask them, "In what ways are these first-century reasons demonstrated in the lives of people today?"

Reaching Conclusions

Every court case comes to an end. The person indicted must be freed or punished; he must be declared innocent or guilty. Either Jesus is the Christ, the Son of the living God, or he is not. What does the evidence show? What conclusion will your students reach? Of what truths will they be able to convince others? These are the primary issues—in any Bible study.

TIME FOR PRAYER

Learning in Praying

by Ronald G. Davis

Prayer is certainly a part of Bible study. We honor God's Word by giving attention to it. We honor its depth and significance by asking for the wisdom of the Spirit in comprehending it and applying it.

Wise teachers of adults will use prayers and praying to enhance every aspect of the class time. Prayers can be read, heard, composed (by tongue or by pen), and sung. The Bible is full of prayers, those spoken as deeply personal responses to God's goodness and those written for the edification and the worship of God's people. Some were written to be read. Some were simply to be heard. Others were designed to be sung. All were to be heartfelt words of worship. Whether they were glad expressions of praise and thanksgiving or desperate, even frantic words of petition, all were an exclamation that God is able.

Prayer With Direction

One of the ways to make certain that prayers focus on elements of thanksgiving and petition that relate to a text and its study is to use "directed prayer." Such prayer means that the leader suggests a series of elements aloud as the praying group utters silent words to the Father.

For a study of Psalm 42, a directed prayer may offer an excellent review and reinforcement of ideas studied. Consider such prayer stimulus statements as the following (with relevant verse numbers in parentheses):

- Pray for hungering and thirsting after righteousness of which Jesus spoke (vv. 1, 2a);
- Pray for ability to make God known to those who say, "Where is your God?" (v. 3);
- Thank God for those with whom you worship and for those who lead worship (v. 4);
- Pray for forgiveness for discouragement and depression; ask for a renewed hope (v. 5);
- Identify to God places and times when you have felt overwhelmed by life's events (vv. 6, 7);
- Address the Father as "God of my life," and ask him to give you his song both day and night (v. 8);
- Plead for steadfastness when the enemies of God taunt and challenge you (vv. 9, 10);

• Affirm the hope that you have; tell God that you praise him for revealing the hope we have in him and in his Son (v. 11).

Closing such a time with oral prayer, in words and phrases from the text, is important. The following statement could be used: "O living God, we have poured out our souls to you. The help of your presence is praiseworthy. Your loving-kindness gives health to our spirits. We thank you for the hope of your abiding Spirit, the hope of resurrection in your Son. Amen."

Prayer With Feet

The concept of prayer walk has an ancient origin; it is reflected in such examples as the "Stations of the Cross" prayer gardens adjoining church buildings of some religious groups. A quiet and serene pathway allowing the discipline of prayer to be practiced has found its way onto modern campgrounds and retreat properties. And it has found simplification in around-the-classroom or around-the-building-hallways manifestations. For such an experience the leader establishes a clearly defined direction of movement and posts prayer-stimulus statements (and, optionally, relevant Bible verses or other spiritual truths) at consecutive (or circular) "stations." Learners are to move from station to station, stopping to pray appropriately at each. Such an activity makes an ideal end-of-unit activity, but it can be applied to individual study occasions.

A lesson taken from Psalm 78 could be the base for an effective "Wonderful Works of God" prayer walk (see vv. 4, 7). A three-part walk could emphasize "Creation—Revelation—Regeneration." Consider for part 1, "Creation," a station carrying the verse Genesis 1:1 and a suggestion to thank God for the very universe of which we are a part, and for its marvelous intricacy and inter-relatedness. Additional "stops" on this part could include "The Plant and Animal Creation," providing us food, clothing, and much more; "Technology," providing us comfort, ease, and breadth of experience; "Medicine," providing strength, health, and extended life; "Art and Beauty," providing us enjoyment, wonder, and an outlet for creativity. The "Revelation" part of the walk could emphasize that which the psalmist emphasizes: that God "decreed statutes . . . and established the law" (v. 5). Using a key verse from that Psalm and an encouragement to thank God for his Word in print could lead to "stops" for thankfulness for translators and translations, publishers, and Christian booksellers.

The contemporary activity most call "prayer walking" is a similar procedure, aimed more at application of truth learned than of review and reinforcement. And prayer walking is done in a life setting rather than a classroom context. Learners are asked to consider a "path" for walking contiguous to the object(s) of the prayer, and they are simply directed to pray as they walk. A lesson from one of many texts in Proverbs, which urges the reader to embrace wisdom, presents an excellent opportunity for a "Wisdom Walk" around a community school or college. The suggestion to walk praying that the students there will find wisdom as well as knowledge is certainly appropriate. (The praying walker could pray for each student he or she passes.) A lesson that encourages proper care for the poor would be an ideal occasion to recommend a walk of prayer through a community of those on the lower end of the socioeconomic scale. Praying for those poor in material things to find obedient faith would be a worthy suggestion.

Prayer with Tunes

Many songs, from ancient hymns to contemporary praise songs, are prayers put into verse and matched to melody. Every adult teacher needs to consider having his or her class sing—or listen to—songs related to lesson texts and themes. (A class member with musical interests might relish the challenge to bring a song or songs to a study session.)

Modern and classic psalters fill shelves of churches and Christian stores. Hymnals typically contain Scripture indexes of the hymns. There are many songs based on Psalm 23; one would be almost remiss if he did not draw attention to one of them. One would be equally remiss if he did not remind the class of the traditional "Old 100th": "All People That on Earth Do Dwell" when Psalm 100 is studied.

Prayer in a Program

The Christian discipline of keeping a prayer journal has proven to be a significant faith-building, disciple-growing practice. Most any Bible study unit can be adapted to a worthy prayer journal—either as a class project or a personal one. In an inexpensive, ruled notebook, with three simple columns: Elements to be Prayed For, Date(s) of the Prayer, and Prayer Responses (with Dates), the user is ready to begin an adventure of Christian growth. Week by week in a study, the teacher and/or the class can list elements related to texts and themes. Day by day the prayers can be offered. Moment by moment the ones who pray can realize the presence and the work of God. Listing prayer content and recording God's gracious response cannot but encourage anyone who seeks him: "The prayer of a righteous person is powerful and effective" (James 5:16).

Prayer Without Ceasing

Try a variety of prayer activities: directed prayer, prayer walks, a prayer list in relationship to a lesson series incorporating elements of praise and petition as a way of unifying and reinforcing the unit, a prayer journal for the unit, writing prayers (and sharing them), reading prayers of others. Prayer changes things, especially the ones who do the praying!

"A Time to Laugh"
Using Humor as a Teaching Tool

by Brent L. Amato

Do your students laugh in your classroom? While teaching is serious business, it should also be fun! Humor helps prime the pump for an effective learning experience. So as teachers strive to create an environment most conducive to learning, humor should not be overlooked.

Some teachers object to this concept. "I am not a humorous person," they say. Or, "I don't know what's funny." Many are afraid they will fail at their attempts at humor and look ridiculous instead. If you are one of those teachers, be encouraged! Everyone has a sense of humor; some are just a bit more hidden than others. With a little effort, you can express your own sense of humor and engage the sense of humor that is in your students.

The How

Here are some tips to consider in developing humor in your teaching:

1. Don't be afraid to move out of your comfort zone. The Holy Spirit prepares your heart to teach, and he also prepares the hearts of your students to learn. This preparation doesn't exclude the use of humor as a teaching aid. Let some of your inhibitions go. But be careful; don't step too far outside your comfort zone. Some things make us uncomfortable because they are in poor taste. Don't sacrifice propriety just for the sake of a laugh.

2. Seize the moment! Some humor will just come naturally, like when you make a mistake or something unexpected or silly happens during the lesson. Don't be afraid to recognize the humor of the moment.

3. Study the art of humor as practiced by others. Watch and learn from teachers and speakers who make their audiences laugh. Good resources are available by Christians noted for their humor. Some examples are Charles Swindoll (*Laugh Again*), Barbara Johnson, and Patsy Clairmont. You can also find books written for public speakers that have funny stories for many topics.

4. While you're studying other people's humor, be sure to tailor your humor to who *you* are. Don't try to mimic others.

5. Make humor part of your lesson plan. Actually script it in.

6. Practice on a spouse or friend. Every well-planned performance has a dress rehearsal.

7. Use humor that is tied to the lesson. You are not there to be a stand-up comedian, cracking jokes just to get a response or to warm up an audience. Humor, like every other part of your lesson, should have the objective of leading your students to an important truth.

8. Avoid humor that is critical of others. I have found that self-deprecating humor is always safe.

9. Use silly, bizarre visual aids. If you cannot draw a perfect map, go ahead and exaggerate the flaws. Just be sure the map still communicates the essential information.

10. Include humorous role-play activities. Many of your students are natural "hams" when in the spotlight.

11. To the extent possible, find humor in biblical situations. For example, Numbers 22 tells the story of Balaam and the talking donkey. Anyone can find humor there! Balaam has what seems to be a stubborn donkey, so he beats it—but then the donkey protests. And Balaam just answers the donkey as if it's the most natural thing in the world for a donkey to talk. Now *that's* funny!

12. Pay attention to current events and news stories that are humorous. You may be able to weave these into your lesson.

The Why

Everyone needs to laugh. Teachers need to laugh. Smiling will always make you more attractive to your students. One manifestation of spiritual health is joy, reflected in part by laughter. Students need to laugh. They not only need minds sharpened with truth, but hearts lifted and lightened by laughter. Your students may remember the fun that they had with you as much as the truth that you taught them.

So don't let a class go by without bringing some smiles and laughter. At those times you will most assuredly have the attention of your students; then teach them!

TOOLS OF THE TRADE

Common Helps for Lesson Preparation

by Brent L. Amato

Just as a master craftsman requires excellent tools for his or her profession, a skilled teacher of the Bible knows about and takes advantage of available resources to enhance each lesson. Imagine yourself starting to prepare your next lesson, with your Bible and lesson commentary open. You want to prepare well; you owe it to the Lord and to your students who are counting on you. What "tools" might help?

Two Spiritual Tools

Resist the temptation to rely only on tools that can be bought in a store or accessed online. There is no substitute for the two spiritual resources that are already on hand for teachers!

The first is the power of the Holy Spirit, who dwells within us (1 Corinthians 6:19). A Spirit-filled teacher will teach a Spirit-filled lesson (Ephesians 3:16). Those blessed with the spiritual gift of teaching should be developing that gift through the power of the Holy Spirit (Romans 12:6, 7). Paul challenged Timothy to give himself wholly to his gift (1 Timothy 4:13-15), and that challenge is ours as well.

The second spiritual tool is prayer. Many times we teachers prepare to teach a biblical passage by studying its technicalities without first spending much time praying about and meditating on that passage. Through prayer we invite God to engage our minds and hearts in the truth of His Word (Psalm 119:18). If that doesn't happen, how can we communicate it properly to our students? It is through prayerful meditation that the Word becomes a way of life to be modeled to our students (Psalm 1:1-3).

We sometimes ignore these tools because they are not something you can put your hands on. It's hard to tell when you are engaging them; they are better seen in hindsight than in the present. So for some, these are impractical: "Just give me three easy steps; don't bother me with this spiritual stuff." Since these tools are spiritual, we sometimes dismiss them as automatic: "God's Spirit will do whatever God's Spirit is going to do—nothing I can do about it!"

But we can do something about it. Paul talks about being filled with the Spirit, of yielding to the Spirit. He also warns of the possibility of grieving the Holy Spirit. We can operate without the Spirit's influence with little or no immediate notice. But if we continue to neglect this aspect of our teaching and of our discipleship, little by little our influence will wane. Our own spiritual fervor will begin to dry up. For our own sakes—to say nothing of our students—we dare not allow that to happen.

Three Man-Made Tools

You're teaching on the humility of Christ from Philippians 2:5-8. You reach into your teacher's toolbox and open a book that lists every passage in the Bible where the word *humility* and its variants appear. You discover more than 70 (KJV) or 100 (NIV) such occurrences you can draw from to enrich your preparation. You've just used a *concordance*!

But wait, your concordance has numbers next to the entries. These are "Strong's numbers," based on a system developed by James A. Strong for his *Exhaustive Concordance to the [King James] Bible*. (Zondervan's *NIV Exhaustive Concordance* has a similar system for the NIV but uses different numbers.) These numbers identify the original Hebrew and Greek words that produce the English words we have in our English Bibles. By looking at the Greek dictionary elsewhere in your concordance, you'll find that these words are sometimes translated differently, and the contexts where those other uses of the words appear will deepen your understanding. For example, the word translated "humility" in James 3:13 is more often translated "gentleness" or a form of that word. This provides some added depth to your understanding of the kind of humility James is talking about here. You don't need a seminary degree to gain insights into the original languages of the Bible when you can use the Strong's (or similar) numbers!

Now suppose you're teaching on Matthew 23, where Jesus pronounces several woes on the *Pharisees*. You wonder who are these guys, anyway? So you reach into your teacher's toolbox, grab a book, and open it to the entry on *Pharisees*, where you read about this sect of Judaism. You've just used a *Bible dictionary*! Sometimes a regular dictionary will help you understand the words in your text. But when the word is about something that hardly comes up outside of a Bible study, a Bible dictionary—or even a Bible encyclopedia—is going to be a much better choice.

Or maybe you're teaching about the special friendship between Jonathan and David, and you read in 1 Samuel 23:15, 16 that "David was . . . in the Desert of Ziph, . . . And Saul's son Jonathan went to David." You reach into your teacher's toolbox and open a book that has a map indicating the location of this wilderness area. Comparing that with Jonathan's starting point, you come away with a much deeper appreciation of Jonathan's journey and, consequently, insight into Jonathan's commitment to David. Your lesson is better illustrated because you've examined a *Bible atlas*!

All these resources, and others as well, are available in print editions, in Bible study software packages, and on the Internet. Most of the online resources are public domain, so they will not contain some of the information that has been learned by archaeologists in recent years, but many of them are still very helpful. Using Bible study software and/or online resources can speed up your study because the computer can search for articles a lot faster than you can!

Don't Let the Tools Get Rusty!

Every time you sit down to prepare to teach, the toolbox should be at your side! It should be ready to be opened and its contents used so that you too "may know the certainty of the things" (Luke 1:4). When you use your tools to that end, your students will end up knowing the things of God as well.

UGLY WORDS, UGLY REALITY
Using Discussion and Debate Effectively

by Ronald G. Davis

It is an ugly word—*schism*—and it is an even uglier reality. *Crisis* compounds the dark picture. And where *schism* and *crisis* are, *confront* must enter. Christ's church was on the line in Corinth. The question was not whether the church would thrive in Corinth, but whether it would survive! The Christians there were letting their differences overwhelm their basic similarity: they were all sinners saved by grace. Some were using sin as a basis for division. Some were using division as an occasion for sin. Paul, by the Holy Spirit, confronted those devilish attitudes with strong words and strong authority.

The differences causing divisions in Corinth were both shallow and deep, both minor and major, both doctrinal and practical. The fulfillment of Jesus' prayer "that all of them may be one" (John 17:21) was being threatened by those divisive elements that separated and threatened to undo the Corinthian church. How could their witness to their pagan world be successful if they showed no unity through a lifestyle of holiness and love?

This was Paul's concern in the first century, and it must be ours in the twenty-first. We must be as unrelenting against disunity in the body of Christ as Paul was. A study of his two epistles to the Corinthians offers a marvelous opportunity to focus on this goal.

Differences need resolution. Doctrines need uniformity. Discussion and debate are teaching strategies that resemble the processes of such resolution and uniformity. Discussion and debate, therefore, are ideal ways to approach such themes.

Discussion is not idle rambling. Nor is it a "mutual exchange of ignorance," as one educator characterized what often happens. Discussion is a planned and prepared-for consideration of issues in which all participants are invited to share personal knowledge, experience, and insights.

Debate, likewise, needs to shed its negative image. In true debate, well-studied speakers address the two opposing sides of a topic. Debate should never consist of attacks on the opponent—only on the weaknesses of one's proposition and argument.

Christians have nothing to fear about honest discussion and debate. Standing on the right side of moral and ethical issues is the only place to be, and that is where Christians must stand.

But we also need an awareness of and a familiarity with the best arguments of those who stand with the devil. Although he is "a liar and the father of lies," as Jesus said (John 8:44), he can be most persuasive.

Discussion Delights

The Corinthian letters feature marvelous blends of the kinds of doctrinal and practical elements that many individuals relish talking about. First Corinthians 7 and 8 are just such studies, beautifully combining doctrine and life.

Paul's simple caution, "Be careful . . . that the exercise of your rights does not become a stumbling block to the weak" (8:9) raises several issues. What adult could resist responding to such a proposition as this: "Stumbling-block arguments are only a thin veil used to cover legalistic faces"? Consider dividing a class into two or more groups to discuss such questions as, "To what extent should the immature influence the decisions of the mature?" "What do love and knowledge have to do with Paul's stumbling-block declaration?" "How is such inappropriate behavior a 'sin against Christ' (8:12)?" "How long should we let another's ignorance keep us from benefiting from our own knowledge?" "How far does Paul's principle, 'If _____ causes my brother to fall into sin, I will never _____,' go?"

Likewise, no matter whether your class is one of singles or couples, old or young, who can ignore a proposition such as this one from 1 Corinthians 7, "The single life is the better life"? As Paul discusses marriage, he boldly declares, "Now to the unmarried and the widows I say: It is good for them to stay unmarried, as I do" (v. 8). Obvious questions surface immediately: "In what ways is the single life to be preferred?" "Is Paul stating an absolute of God or a purely personal view?" "God's design from the beginning was 'A man will leave his father and mother and be united to his wife, and the two will become one flesh' (Matthew 19:5); how does Paul's teaching relate to that?" "How do some of Paul's other affirmations about marriage and divorce in 1 Corinthians 7 relate to contemporary culture?"

Discussion will enliven the class, if the questions asked are personally and culturally relevant. The teacher's task is to write the questions and to invite class members to give them some thought before the discussion takes place. Whether that is accomplished by distributing a copy of all the questions ahead of time or simply by asking various members to be "primed" to deal with one particular question, the method of preparation is unimportant. That the preparation happens is critical.

Debate Dichotomies

Debate is a form of discussion, but it is more formalized. Control is exercised over time, order of speakers, and opportunity for audience participation. Whether it involves one individual versus another or one team versus another team, debate produces a clear-cut division between the parties involved. A debate has the potential, as it unfolds, to raise some hackles. Debate, to be fully effective, needs to elicit some emotion—the emotion of strongly held belief, realizing what is at stake in peoples' lives.

A study of 1 Corinthians 13 provides an opportunity to highlight the difference between a cynical perspective and a godly one. To many in the modern world, the loving lifestyle is a foolish, even fatal, one. Think what could ensue if you divided your class into "Cynics" and "Believers" and asked them to prepare arguments for and against this proposition: "Resolved: the loving lifestyle, as beautiful as it sounds, will not work in the contemporary world!" You may want to give the class a week to prepare for this debate. Consider distributing your lesson outline to help participants in their preparation.

When the class session begins, give the two sides a brief time to meet and to compile their "arguments." Have each select a spokesperson (or two) for its position. Give each speaker a limited time (two to three minutes), alternate, allow class participation orally at the end, then summarize the issues raised and the conclusions drawn.

The role of the Spirit in daily living and in the revelation of truth has been deliberated from the first century to the present. Thus, a study of any text that includes the work of the Spirit can be a good one to employ debate. In a study of 1 Corinthians 2, such a resolution as the following could lead to an edifying debate: "The inspiration of the Spirit in the preparation of infallible documents is at the core of my faith." Some believe that inspiration of Scripture is a fuzzy doctrine for fuzzy minds. Even more avow that infallibility is meaningless, and thus unimportant, since we do not possess any of the original manuscripts of the New Testament.

As your class arrives for the study, hand out "Inspired" and "Uninspired" labels alternately. (Consider also distributing a list of Scriptures on the topic.) Again, let each group meet and develop its statements. This time you may want to alternate 30-second statements from the two sides, asking members to stand and be recognized before they speak. (This will work better if you seat the two groups so that they are facing each other.)

Sometimes, to encourage clarity in thinking, it is good to let groups or individuals prepare for one side, then present the other side's arguments! (They will need a brief period of time to consider the *written* notes of the other side.)

Now take a look at 2 Corinthians 2:4-17. Which of the following resolution statements do you believe could best be debated in your class?

1. The best way to deal with troublemakers is forgiveness and encouragement.
2. Confrontation is sometimes necessary, even when it brings grief.
3. The Christian must serve as the fragrance of life to those who are saved, but as the smell of death to the unsaved (cf. 2 Corinthians 2:15, 16).

What arguments or questions would you suggest to your debaters in order to examine the statement to be debated? How would you organize the classroom and the procedure for your debate?

The Corinthian church could be characterized as one with ugly words and ugly behaviors. What Paul wanted (and what God wanted) was the beauty of holiness and unity. What could be better goals for today's church? For our church? Will we let cracks become canyons? Will we let fences become fortresses? Or will we work for that holiness and unity for which Christ prayed and died?

USING SMALLER GROUPS
IN AND OUT
OF THE CLASSROOM
Enhancing Relationships Among Class Members

by Brett DeYoung

In adult education, it is important to use a variety of group sizes to help facilitate learning. There is a need for adults to be in a large group, like a worship service where it is a safe place to participate only as one feels comfortable. This group we will call a church-size group. The next size group is a class-size group. It is a group that is generally larger than 12 people. This is a place were one can learn and build casual relationships with others without becoming too vulnerable. In this setting a person can feel free to give his opinions and ask questions, but also feel safe enough that he will not have to participate in reading Scripture, answering Bible questions, or sharing in the discussion unless he wants to do so.

The next group is a circle-size group. It is a group of 12 or fewer. This group is the place where each person is free to share in dialogue and vulnerability. It becomes the perfect place for people to share deeper needs, encourage one another, and give comments they may not be willing to share in the class-size or church-size groups.

Using Smaller Groups in the Classroom

Use small groups in a variety of ways during a class period. Try using them to grab interest at the beginning of the lesson or to reinforce the application at the end.

How do you divide a class into groups? Number off to make random groups, or let people form their own groups by saying, "Please divide into groups no larger than six—and try to choose people you normally don't talk with." Sometimes it may be appropriate to have men-only and women-only groups. If your class sits at tables, you may simply use the groups that naturally form that way. If you want to mix them up, since people tend to sit in the same place week in and week out, you can say, "Let's mix up our groups a bit; I need two people from each table to find a new table to sit at—and the two may not go to the same table."

Be creative in selecting the groups' facilitators. People may resist being a "leader," so make it appear fun and not burdensome. The leader can be the person who has received the most speeding tickets, the person born farthest from the church building, the person whose birthday is closest to today, the person wearing the most blue, the person with the largest shoe size, or any other such random designation.

After a few minutes of group discussion, how do you recapture the class's attention? Try saying, "I'm sorry to break in, but I need to have your attention." Many times the groups will continue and not pay any attention to a leader, so try, "Hello, is anyone out there? May I please have your attention?" After you gain their attention, allow the groups to share what they learned. Have in mind how long you can spend for this and give as many students as you can an opportunity to share. If it is difficult to get this discussion started, choose someone who is outgoing or a couple of the leaders to tell you what they observed.

Be considerate of first-time guests; they may be uncomfortable leading a small group discussion. Encourage everyone to share something, but also let newcomers know it's OK if they don't participate. Be extra sensitive and do not use questions or ideas that are too personal.

When using smaller groups within an adult class, try to limit the group sizes to six or less. This enables people to get to know one another and allows each member to participate in the discussion.

A small group encounter will work best if the group members are physically positioned close to one another. It helps when each participant can observe facial expressions and body language and hear comments clearly. If small groups sit in circles, be careful not to leave anyone outside the circle. Let people know that it's OK to move the furniture if needed.

Remember that variety is the key to any method of teaching. Be careful not to overdo small groups or make a change only for the sake of change.

Using Smaller Groups Outside the Classroom

The key to a successful small-group ministry outside the classroom is securing and training good leaders. Look for **FAT** Christians—those who are Faithful, Available, and Teachable. Can you count on them? Will they do what they say? When life becomes complicated, will they still be leading the group or will they have moved on to the next opportunity? Do they have a teachable spirit, or do they think they know all there is to know?

Each group leader should recruit an assistant or apprentice who can share in the group's ministry. The assistant can share in leading the group's discussion and prayer needs. This apprenticeship also provides a way to expand when the group is growing too large and is ready to give birth to a new group. Where do leaders find assistant leaders? Search among friends in class or at church. Don't rule out family members, people you enjoy being with socially, or people with whom you work.

Small groups, in most situations, work best in the warm and relaxed atmosphere of a home. However, other locations, such as restaurants, corporate conference rooms, or even the church building can also be good places to meet. The first impression, the first time the group meets, sets the tone for the meetings to follow. It is important to start and end on time.

A good way to help a group get started in the right direction is to use a group covenant. This is an agreement that each member is asked to sign (or in some other way express acceptance of its terms and responsibilities). A group covenant can include the following:

A. The purpose of the group.

B. The study materials, including the cost if applicable.

C. The version of the Bible to be used.

D. Meeting day and time.

E. Meeting location(s).

F. Agenda and schedule.

G. Length of commitment (after which the group will be evaluated).

H. How childcare will be handled.

I. A commitment to confidentiality.

Childcare can be the biggest headache for parents wanting to be in a small group. If meeting in a large home, the adults can meet in one area while the children play in another. This works best if an older sibling, baby-sitter, or adult supervises the children's activities. If adults are used, be sure to rotate the responsibilities. Dropping the children at another person's home (someone who is not in the group but agrees to provide the childcare) also can work. Senior citizens may wish to help, or the church's youth may want the opportunity to raise support for youth outings or upcoming mission trips by working as permanent baby-sitters for your group.

Lyman Coleman, a long-time advocate for small groups in the church, illustrates a small group experience with a picture of a baseball diamond. He calls home plate "true fellowship," which can happen after a group successfully goes around each of the bases. First base is all about *history giving*. People in the group tell their stories to each other. These stories include their childhood experiences, heritage, spiritual journey, and hopes and dreams for the future. Second base is achieved when group members give *affirmation* to each other by giving each person a chance to respond to the group's stories. Group members receive encouragement from each other. Third base represents *goal setting* for the individuals in the group. This may be the place where they decide what they need to do next to become all that God wants them to be.

Creating small groups from among your class members is an excellent way to support the ministry of the class. Relationships are enhanced in these small settings, but the stronger relationships thus formed increase the power of the interaction in your class. Meeting mid-week, group members can follow up on things discussed on Sunday and encourage application of the principles learned. This kind of small group interaction begins to transform your larger group from an academic "class" to a caring, sharing, growing "community" of disciples.

Many churches use small groups as a means for Bible study, fellowship, and ministry during the week. If your church is one of them, then you will need to work with the leadership to establish the small groups from within your class. Some of your students may already belong to small groups, and creating new groups could wreak havoc on the program. But most small group programs have regular time for realigning of groups. Use such times to create the groups that will support your class's ministry.

VARIETY IS THE SPICE OF TEACHING

Involving All the Senses

by Charlotte Mize

Teaching is an enormous but rewarding responsibility. Many people are fearful of becoming teachers because teachers bear a greater accountability (James 3:1). However, there are also admonitions for followers of Christ to mature spiritually to the point where they can teach others (Titus 2:3; Hebrews 5:12). God honors those who teach (Romans 10:15).

Better Teaching, Greater Learning

When a kindergarten teacher begins to show her class how to read, she doesn't read all of the material to them. She allows them to struggle with the letters, the sounds, the words, and finally the sentences. She provides a learning experience where children can develop their own skills. The teacher is the guide and the role model, but she does not do all the work for the child.

Adults need a similar environment—an environment that allows them to mature in their faith. It is your job as teacher to create such an environment. You provide the gift (lesson), but you don't unwrap it entirely for your learners. You allow them the excitement of discovery.

One phrase that has stuck with me from my early days of teaching is this: "There is no teaching without parallel learning, and there is no learning without a change in behavior." For bringing about behavioral change, the lecture method is probably the least effective. One reason for that is that lecture uses only one of the learner's five senses: hearing. A challenge for teachers is to find ways to engage more than one of the five senses.

For example, merely talking about the ark of the covenant can be abstract and dull. Seeing a picture of the ark brings some interest. Making a model of the ark based on God's instructions to Moses (Exodus 25) will involve even more senses. (Use simple materials to keep the model-building manageable within the time available.)

For a lesson from 1 Chronicles 17, you can challenge each class member to write some kind of brief contract (covenant). This can be a sales contract, a neighborhood watch pact, or some other agreement. A key point is that the expectations of all parties should be clear. For a study of the building of Solomon's temple (1 Chronicles 28, 29; 2 Chronicles 2–5) the class can research Solomon's temple and bring samples of the building and decorating materials (or pictures downloaded from the Internet, if samples are hard to come by).

Studying Solomon's dedication of the temple (2 Chronicles 6:12-17) can involve a dramatic monologue to reenact Solomon's prayer of dedication. Thinking about Josiah's renewing of the covenant (2 Chronicles 34), one application activity is to have your class brainstorm what a rededication ceremony for your church would involve.

Don't overlook the importance of visualization and role-playing; these can affect the subconscious. For example, in a lesson from Daniel 1, you can write a very short three-act play to involve the entire class in the story of the young Hebrew men's standing up for what is right in the midst of persecution. A parallel play based on a modern situation will allow your learners to see how the lesson applies today.

Write the fiery message of Daniel 3 on learners' hearts as well as on their minds with active, intense visualization. Have a reader dramatically speak the lesson text while everyone has eyes closed. Challenge learners to hear, feel, see, and smell the atmosphere of that episode as they visualize the progression.

A lesson from Daniel 6 invites a comparison between the lions' den of Daniel's persecution and the Roman persecution of Christians. Then you can share modern stories of persecution of Christians. The Voice of the Martyrs Web site (www.persecution.com) can provide you some good material.

Daniel prays for the people in chapter 9. This would be a good time for a real-life experience. The class can select a section of town where there is much evil and pray for the people there. The best involvement would be to go to the area, but an alternative would be for the class to divide into groups in the classroom to pray using Daniel's prayer as a pattern. The prayer certainly should include confession for not doing more as a church to reach that area for Christ.

The book of Haggai provides some great texts for lessons on setting priorities. For such a study, cut out articles and advertisements from a week's worth of newspapers. As you pass them around for discussion on how to avoid being influenced by worldly priorities, you will be engaging the eyes, the ears, and the sense of touch.

A study of Nehemiah offers an opportunity to invite some of your church leaders to share with the class their vision for how to improve the church facilities to reach more for Jesus. Especially if your text includes Nehemiah 2:11-15, arrange for those leaders to take your class on a walking tour of the church facility either during class or later. Class members may find themselves motivated to volunteer for a service activity during the ensuing week to further that vision. Make time in a later lesson to hear reports from some who were motivated to volunteer for service as a result of this activity.

For a study of Nehemiah 8, think of a way to arrange your classroom space that parallels the arrangement during Ezra's reading of the law. As your learners stand to hear, a prepared volunteer can read the Ten Commandments (Deuteronomy 5:1-21) or the Beatitudes (Matthew 5:1-13).

Trying to reproduce Ezra's high platform indoors is probably neither feasible nor safe. But something that allows the speaker to stand safely at least a few inches off the floor can add to the dramatic effect. Some of your learners should be prepared to respond *amen, amen* and adopt the various postures noted in Nehemiah 8:6. The people weren't passive when Ezra read the law!

Don't Forget the Overall Theme

Sometimes we focus just on each lesson, but it's important to keep the big picture in mind as well. Nearly every lesson occurs as part of a series or unit of lessons that has some theme that unifies the lessons. All of the examples above came from a series that dealt with the concept of *covenant* in one way or another. In teaching such a series, it is vital for teacher and learner to understand what is involved in a covenant, since this involves understanding how various relationships work.

To introduce a series on covenant, ask your class to try to think of some human interactions that involve a covenant or agreement, either formally or informally. How are those similar to God's covenant with us? How are they different?

If your learners need help, you can offer modern examples of covenants such as business contracts and marriage vows. Point out that *covenant* implies some kind of agreement between at least two parties, although the parties may not be equals. The words *treaty, pact, accord,* or *contract* may be more familiar to your learners than *covenant.*

If your learners need more examples from you, you can mention that parents use covenants (contracts) with their children to define expected behavior and what rewards and punishments are included. God understands the need his children have for covenant. The Bible is the story of the unfolding of God's covenants with his people throughout history. Throughout the series, review often the concept of covenant so that the overall theme does not get lost in individual stories.

Your learners also need to know that covenants demand faithfulness on both sides. God is faithful. His children must grow in their faithfulness. God made a covenant with his chosen nation, Israel. God remained faithful to all his promises in both reward and punishment. His nation was not faithful and thus often suffered the punishment.

However, God also made provision for restoration. The church, unfortunately, has been unfaithful at times. Like the nation of Israel in the Old Testament, we sometimes need restoration. Restoration is available through Jesus' sacrifice and payment for our sin (1 John 1:9).

Human-to-human agreements will end, but our new covenant with God is everlasting. Even when we fail, the covenant continues. This is the only eternal agreement. It is reassuring to know that God's covenant will never fail. Make sure that your learners realize that the new covenant in Jesus is *our* hope.

Don't Be Afraid to be Creative

Finding creative ways to allow learners to discover God's truth is a challenge. Start by asking yourself, "How can I involve as many of the five senses as possible in my next lesson?"

The advance planning needed to do this may seem to be too time-consuming. At first it will take additional time to prepare an effective learning environment thoughtfully. But with practice this becomes easier, even second nature. The results will be gratifying.

"WELL, WHAT DO YOU KNOW?"
The Importance of Content

by Ronald G. Davis

Educators are sometimes accused of being more concerned about content than about life. That accusation, perhaps occasionally justified, often overlooks one basic truth: life decisions are made from a cognitive foundation. What one knows (and doesn't know) strongly affects his or her behavioral decisions.

Poor choices—even sinful choices—often come as a result of either inadequate knowledge or erroneous "knowledge." Perhaps one doesn't know enough of God's truth. Or maybe he or she has believed a lie and mistaken it for the truth.

Teacher preparation for a lesson session must early include two questions: (1) "What do my learners know about the content at hand?" and (2) "What do they need to know to make better life decisions?"

Adult teachers, especially of long-running study groups, may proceed with the (wrong) assumption that the students already know the content of the typical Bible lesson. (If they do, then they need to be studying something deeper!) But sincere Bible students want to know more and more about the character and the plan of God, the history of his people, and the application of godliness to daily life. In this light the teacher's first goal is to establish a firm cognitive base for the students. This will allow them to develop godly attitudes and behaviors.

Truths to be known, resulting in faith to be affirmed, leading to right living to be blessed—that is why we all teach. No teacher need apologize for emphasizing knowledge of the Bible and Bible backgrounds.

The Background

Historical and geographical settings characterize truth. Myth and folklore are set in "once upon a time" and "countries far away." The Bible is set in real times and real places. Fiction creates people (and lesser creatures) to do the whims of the author. Truth records the deeds of real people. Understanding the culture of the biblical story helps one understand the Bible texts and the Bible people.

Seeing how individuals lived their daily lives—through their hopes, fears, and aspirations—and how they responded to the good news of Christ helps the contemporary person make right decisions.

Introducing your students to some typical residents of Jesus' first-century Galilee and Judea and the wider Roman world is important in New Testament lessons. To do this, consider using an occasional dramatic monologue. Possibilities include a Christian living in Colosse when Paul's letter arrives, a Roman centurion stationed in Palestine, a Judean shepherd, a believing Jew, a Galilean peasant present at the feeding of the thousands, and a vine grower.

Perhaps a member of your class or congregation who enjoys drama would like to write his or her own monologue. This requires a diligent study of texts and commentary sources. About 300 to 400 words is needed for a three-minute presentation. Here is a sample for a shepherd, a "bad" shepherd, which could be used as background for Luke 2, John 10, or some other "shepherd" text:

Yeah, I'm one of those "bad" shepherds you hear about in the big city of Jerusalem. If we shepherds do our jobs well, no one notices. When our sheep are sold for sacrifice, the buyer is looking forward not backward. When our sheep become someone's tasty meal, thoughts of our work are "swallowed" along with the meat.

But I've heard all the snide remarks: "Wouldn't trust him as far as I could throw the temple." Our reputation precedes us from field to field. Sure, they trust us with their sheep, but step out of the field and we're suspected of everything: thievery, drunkenness, profanity, irreverence. We end up dirty, smelly, tired, and hungry.

So perhaps our manners don't quite match the standards of the Pharisees. We don't rightly care a fig. And maybe we don't get to the synagogue as often as we should. But those sheep don't protect themselves, don't water themselves, don't find new grass for themselves—even on the Sabbath.

Perhaps a Pharisee could come out and watch the sheep while we go to the synagogue! Ha! I'll see that the day the Messiah comes, greets me by name, and says, 'Say, friend, I'm a shepherd too. Let me watch the sheep while you rest for a while!'

Obviously geography is a part of every lesson as well. From the towns and villages around the Sea of Galilee to the city of Jerusalem, Jesus lived and served in real places. Maps of those areas around the sea and the city will significantly support your learners' understanding of the context of his teaching. John is very careful to indicate Jesus' location, which varies from Galilee to Jerusalem and back to Galilee. Two basic learning principles for maps are size and interactivity.

Because the Sea of Galilee is only about 12 miles from north to south and about 6 miles at its widest, a wall of your room can become a "one foot = two miles" map, or six feet by three feet, very easily. The sea on your map should approximate the shape of an upside down pear.

Use stick-on labels to designate places of Jesus' teaching. For example the site of the Feeding of the 5,000 is on the northeast shore. This geographical context will help students see the way Jesus and his disciples sailed across the sea before the people ran around the shore to meet him on "the other side" near Capernaum. Let students guess and measure the distances, given the simple scale.

You can use a scanner to capture a drawing of Jerusalem to create an overhead transparency or a computer-projected image. This will promote a clearer concept of Jesus' movements around the city at various times. Your discussion can include his birth in Bethlehem, only a few miles to the south. You can also point out the temple and nearby Bethany when your lesson texts call for it. Students may not realize that the Jerusalem of Jesus' day was little more than one mile square; overlaying that with your local street grid can be insightful.

Any pictorial material of Israel, in any format, that you use to decorate your room will help students confirm the reality of Jesus' places.

The Word

With every lesson the Scripture text is a starting point. Seeing it, reading it, and hearing it should be "givens" for the students. The old-fashioned strategy of letting students read one verse at a time in sequence around the group may be a novel idea in contemporary classrooms. But your class probably has some who are excellent oral readers; you will want to use those God-given talents as well. Also consider letting students hear the text read professionally from a prerecorded format. These are available in Christian stores and online.

In a lesson series that emphasizes one writer, seeing the repeated use of key words and terms will have a cumulative effect that is nothing but positive. You might like to keep a running tally of the times certain key words are used from lesson to lesson. Put up a large sheet of paper with the heading "John's Frequent Words," for example. List several, such as *light, darkness, life, know, word, God, Father, world, truth.* Mark the times the words are found week to week. Your learners will be surprised how emphatically repetitious John is!

Because John uses the same words repeatedly, your class may enjoy and appreciate an introduction to some of the Greek language words that stand behind those frequent uses. For example when Jesus calls himself "the light of the world," the Greek for "light" is *phos* (pronounced *fos* with a long *o*) while the Greek for "world" is *cosmos.* These two Greek words form the basis of some common English words: *photograph* and *cosmic* are just two examples. If you don't have skills in Greek personally, a Bible dictionary will help.

Never Too Much

Your students can never know too much Scripture nor too much about Scripture. God's Word is deep and wide. Scholars have plumbed those depths and widths for centuries. Ordinary Bible students have delighted in its riches from the time Moses began writing it down by God's Spirit.

As Paul insists, "All Scripture is God-breathed and is useful for teaching, rebuking, correcting and training in righteousness, so that the servant of God may be thoroughly equipped for every good work" (2 Timothy 3:16, 17). The diligent teacher of adults will never stop asking the students, "Well, what do you know?"

"WHAT CAN I LEARN FROM HISTORY?"

Lessons from the Gospel of Luke

by Richard A. Koffarnus

Many people talk about the subject of history in negative terms. "History is more or less bunk," said Henry Ford (1863–1947). "History is little else than a picture of human crimes and misfortunes," complained the French philosopher Voltaire (1694–1778).

Those who study and preserve history are also frequent targets of condemnation. "Historians," one anonymous critic wrote, "fall into one of three categories: those who lie, those who are mistaken, and those who do not know."

Yet without history and the historians who record it, we would be ignorant of the roots of our culture. Without that knowledge, society would have to rediscover its foundations and core principles constantly. For that reason, even the most primitive peoples, often without a written language, employ tribal historians to pass on their oral traditions.

The New Testament gives us some historical perspective in the Gospels and the book of Acts. Through a study of one or more of the Gospels and the book of Acts, you can challenge your learners to broaden their historical knowledge of the New Testament era. The following examples will come from the Gospel of Luke—though the principles will work with any historical book of the Bible. Luke was author both of the third Gospel and the book of Acts, the inspired historical account of the first 30 years of the church. A physician by trade, Luke was a traveling companion and coworker of Paul.

Understanding Historical Context

One way to make history relevant to your learners is to put your lesson material into a historical context. When did the events recorded in the text actually take place?

Many chronologies of the life of Christ exist. For example, the *Standard Bible Atlas* contains such a chronology, as does *A Harmony of the Gospels* by Robert Thomas and Stanley Gundry. J.W. McGarvey's *Fourfold Gospel* is also a helpful blending of the four Gospels into one chronological story. A much shorter and very colorful tool that does much the same thing is Standard Publishing's

Discovering God's Story. You can use reference tools such as these to prepare a time line to display each week. That way your class will always know where they are in their study of the life of Christ.

You can also help your learners understand historical context by answering the question, "What was going on in the world at the time of these events?" Each week have a different student report on some notable historical event that took place between 6 BC and AD 30, the time period covered in Luke's Gospel. Besides describing the events, each report should answer the question, "What relationship, if any, did this event have to life in first-century Israel?" Check your local library and the Internet for historical information on this time period.

Another way to make history relevant to your learners is to let them "witness" it happening. There are several good video portrayals of the Gospel of Luke available, including *The Jesus Film*. Most have narration taken directly from Luke. They strive to recreate the authentic look and feel of first-century Israel as Jesus experienced it. You can show a relevant clip from the video to introduce each lesson so your learners can form accurate mental pictures of the people, places, and events described by Luke. (Make sure not to violate copyrights. NEST Entertainment has a variety of animated Bible stories, and permission to show to a group is automatic with purchase.)

Studying History's Superstars

An approach once commonly used by historians, including Luke, is the so-called "great-man theory" of history. According to this approach, we can discover the causes of the great events of the past by studying the important people of history. Of course, Luke focuses his work on the greatest historical figure of them all, the Lord Jesus.

Still, there are other notables worth learning about who appear in the third Gospel. The Roman Emperor Augustus is mentioned by Luke as part of the background to the birth of Christ in chapter 2. How much do your learners actually know about this powerful ruler and his impact on the Mediterranean world? One way to enlighten them would be to have a class member portray him by delivering a monologue about his life. Another possibility is to have two learners pretend to be angels in conversation about the shocking contrast between the luxurious lifestyle of Augustus and the humble birth of the King of kings.

Later in Luke's gospel we encounter the familiar figure of Pontius Pilate. Nearly everyone knows the role Pilate played in the crucifixion of Christ, but few know anything else about his life and work in first-century Israel. How did he come to power? What kind of governor was he? What became of him after the resurrection of Jesus?

To enhance a report on Pilate, you can post several pictures of this Roman that are based on his theorized likeness as taken from coins and artwork (easy to find on the Internet). Include the caption, "Have you seen this man?" Pretend that you (or one of your learners) are a TV news reporter presenting a missing-person case to your viewers. Discuss the rise and fall of Pilate in history and legend. Explain what we know and don't know about the fate of the man who executed Jesus.

Learning About the Less-than-Greats

In recent years, the "great-man theory" of history has been replaced among historians by other approaches. One of the newer approaches deals with social history. Instead of focusing only on the big-shot "movers and shakers" of society, many historians now want to know what the less-than-great people were thinking and doing.

The theory here is that more often than not history's great leaders respond to changes among the masses rather than the other way around. The social historian is interested in why such developments happened when they did and what effects they later had.

Although Luke was not a social historian, he gives us numerous glimpses of first-century Palestinian culture in his story of Jesus. Properly highlighted, these "snapshots" can help your class to understand better the significance of what Jesus was teaching and doing.

For example, in chapter 1 we meet John the Baptist's father, a priest named Zechariah. We learn from an appearance of the angel Gabriel that John is to be raised as a Nazarite, never tasting wine or strong drink. Your learners will gain a clearer perspective of this if they understand something of the work of a temple priest and the lifestyle and practices of a Nazarite. During class, you can "interview" two learners—one portraying a priest and the other a Nazarite—to explain what each one does and why he does it. Some of your learners may enjoy doing the advance research required for such a role play.

In Luke 14 Jesus attends a Sabbath day banquet in the home of a prominent Pharisee. Jesus used the seating customs associated with such a banquet to teach on the nature of true humility. To illustrate this setting, arrange your classroom like a first-century banquet room, with the chairs arranged in the shape of a "U" or a semi-circle. Reserve one chair in the middle for yourself and two chairs on either side of it for "honored guests." After your learners have seated themselves, move some to places of greater honor and some to lesser places.

Before class, explain the exercise to the learners being demoted so they can pretend to be humiliated. For the most realism, you can use floor cushions (instead of chairs) arranged around a very low table, although this may not be practical for various reasons.

Other customs mentioned by Luke include the presentation of the infant Jesus at the temple (Luke 2:21-40) and the celebration of Passover (Luke 2:41-52; 22:1-20). To research these topics, you can consult Bible dictionaries and encyclopedias or books devoted to Bible customs. Of course, the Internet is a great research tool as well.

Twenty-Twenty Hindsight

Modern Christians have the advantage of being able to look back at completed events of salvation-history that the Old Testament prophets could only imagine (1 Peter 1:10-12). History is far from being "bunk"! Most Christians would agree that history is, in reality, "his story"—the workings of God in human affairs.

That being the case, we can only benefit from a greater understanding of the historical context of the New Testament, since that knowledge will help us to interpret and apply God's Word correctly. History thus becomes a window on the present and future work of God. As the French poet and politician Alphonse De Lamartine (1790 –1869) observed, "Providence conceals itself in the details of human affairs, but becomes unveiled in the generalities of history."

WHEN TO USE THE LECTURE METHOD

And When Not to Use It

by James Riley Estep, Jr.

Lecture is one of the most ancient and reliable methods of adult instruction. While some have pronounced the lecture dead in the contemporary classroom, it is still used effectively in universities, seminars, etc. It does have its problems; it does not help students learn to think for themselves, for example. But the lecture still can be the preferred method of instruction in certain situations.

When to Use the Lecture Method

The lecture method is ideal for *transmitting information*. Other methods assist in processing information or challenging students to action. But lecture is often the best way to transmit information in a short amount of time. Thus, lecture may be appropriate . . .

When information is not readily available to the student from another source. The teacher may study a topic that is unknown or obscure to the students.

When the teacher needs to synthesize information from a variety of sources. The teacher will often study several commentaries on a Bible passage. He can thus combine the information and explain why different interpretations exist.

When the teacher needs to highlight relationships and points that students may not recognize. It is easy to overlook facts from one part of the Bible when studying another part.

To deepen the student's motivation to learn additional information. Lecture can be used to raise questions in the student's mind, causing him or her to seek answers. Teachers promote this kind of seeking when not providing "the" definitive answer to the question at hand.

If there is a need to correct a misunderstanding of the Bible or doctrine. For example, Mormon doctrine teaches that Jesus and Satan are brothers. The lecture method can be used to make students aware of this teaching and to refute it.

To remove obstacles to learning, such as inadequate or wrong assumptions. For example, Bible students have developed many assumptions about the book of Revelation. Lecture can provide insight into the assumptions before delving into the text itself.

To resolve conflicting perspectives on a given subject or text. Lecture can be used to explain opposing viewpoints. This may provide an opportunity to search for common ground among those viewpoints.

When the teacher's personality is best seen in a lecture. Teaching is a very personal activity. Lecture often allows the student to go beyond the content of the lesson to learn from the teacher's life.

Thus the lecture method remains a legitimate teaching method. However, this not to suggest that lecture is the only valid method of instruction.

When *Not* to Use the Lecture Method

There are at least four factors that should cause the teacher to consider using a method other than straight lecture. Lecture may not be appropriate . . .

If your learning objectives require you to go beyond mastery of content. Every lesson should feature not only a content lesson aim, but also concept and conduct aims. Your learners need to go beyond what the Bible says to what it means and, especially, what it *demands* of your learners. These aims will usually be best accomplished through some means other than lecture.

If your class has knowledgeable students who can contribute insight to the subject at hand. For example, why lecture about global missions if your class happens to have a former missionary?

If you have time to use more creative teaching methods. Once when I was teaching at an adult retreat, I literally had hours of time to fill. That amount of time was ideal for me to use teaching methods other than lecture.

If your classroom is not designed for lecture. If your learning area is equipped with chairs at round tables, with a projector and no lectern, etc., then why force a lecture method into a physical context not designed for it?

In short, lecture is a good method, but not the only good method. Recognizing the times and places that make lecture useful is as important as knowing what other methods are available for those times and places when it is not.

YES OR NO?

The Eternal Choice

by Ronald G. Davis

Sometimes our lessons are based on specific texts as we study a book of the Bible. Other lessons are more topical in nature, perhaps tied to events or issues of particular relevance. Another plan of study is to do character studies. In many ways the Bible is a record of people who said yes or no to God's call. Though we have a tendency to picture people in literature and in the Bible one-dimensionally, the people on the sacred page are real people. They are a blend of inconsistencies—of knowledge and ignorance, of discernment and foolishness, of objectivity and emotionalism. They are, in fact, just like us. Some will cry, "Yes!" with vigor; some will stutter, "Y-y-yes," with trepidation. A few will boldly and foolishly blurt, "No!" Some will say nothing, and their silence will register as a no. As we diligently compare and contrast them with God's ideal, with one another, and with ourselves, we want ourselves and our learners to learn how to say "Yes" to God unreservedly.

Is It a Yes or a No?

One of the ways to see the multifaceted humanness of a Bible character is to decide what attributes can be appropriately applied. Give the learners a sheet of attributes, evenly spaced in two columns on a page, with the directions that the sheet be folded and torn (or cut) into separate pieces, each with one descriptor. Then ask the learners to make two piles: a "yes" pile and a "no" pile. The yes pile will contain all the attributes appropriate to the person; the no pile, the inappropriate ones.

As an example, try the following list of adjectives and nouns for the apostle Peter (with sample references for discussion): *brusque, confident* (Luke 22:33), *cowardly, deceitful, faithful, foolish, Galilean, humble, impulsive, jealous, liar* (Luke 22:56, 57), *lonely, sensitive, self-deceived, repentant*. Once everyone has established two piles, compare and contrast the results. Let learners explain why they have placed any words differently from others.

Paul would make an interesting second choice for such an activity. Such words (with sample references for discussion) as the following could be useful: *bold, content, fearful, fearless, humble, impartial* (Acts 26:22), *Jewish, law-abiding* (Acts 26:12), *obedient, persuasive, preju-diced, unprepared, violent, zealous.* A richer, fuller concept of the person under study should emerge.

Such a look at a negative example of faith could be interesting as well. Try the rich man of Mark 10:17-22 with the following descriptors. (Be sure to have your learners looking also at the parallel passages in Matthew 19:16-22 and Luke 18:18-23.) Descriptors for the attributes sheet may include the following: *deceitful, demanding, eager, generous, gentile, Heaven-bound, joyful, lovable, mistaken, old, perceptive, rich, rude, self-confident.* As in any occasion of using such an activity, there will be disagreement for several as to whether they truly represent the man. But that disagreement will allow a helpful discussion of the text and the person.

A teacher may have a class that would like to approach such an activity in a more composi-tional way. Give each learner a sheet with the heading, "_____ was definitely. . . ." (Fill in the blank with the name of the Bible character you want to study.) Below that, have ten rectangles in two columns of five. Direct the class to fill in ten attributes or character traits of the character named, one per box. When boxes are filled, have class members swap sheets with one another and explain their different choices.

Can I Say Yes?

Of course, one of the reasons the Spirit has highlighted certain people in biblical history is so that women and men in every generation and in every geography can see the Spirit at work—either being welcomed and nurtured or being rejected and quenched. It behooves the Bible student to compare and contrast himself with the individuals coming face to face with God's truth in biblical settings. A simple, personal yes-or-no response to the behaviors of lesson heroes and heroines helps the fruit of the Spirit to ripen.

Priscilla and Aquila, Christian wife and husband, are interesting subjects of study. Consider giving your class—either in print or orally—a series of statements characterizing their godly life-style, asking students to respond yes or no to each. (If done orally, you are asking only for medita-tive, silent responses.) Use statements such as these: (1) I carry my faith with me everywhere I go; (2) My vocation serves the noble needs of fellow citizens; (3) I welcome people into my home in the spirit of hospitality; (4) I encourage Christian evangelists and missionaries on their way; (5) My house is open and available to the functions of the church; (6) My commitment to the success of the gospel is long-term; (7) I am confident enough and bold enough to correct one who misrepresents the gospel; (8) I will "stick my neck out" for a brother or sister under attack; (9) I have a good repu-tation among the churches where I am known; (10)—For married learners—My spouse and I are united in godly priority. During the introduction or the conclusion, you may want to discuss how each of these statements was true of Priscilla and Aquila; for example, take a look at Acts 18:24-26 in reference to number 7.

Similar statements might be prepared and used for other characters, such as Timothy. Statements that could be used for him include the following. (1) I learned the gospel from a believing mother; (2) I never use my family background as an excuse to avoid ministry; (3) I have a good reputation locally; (4) I submit readily to that which is expedient, even if it is not essential; (5) I can "play second fiddle" to a strong leader; (6) My goal is to extend Christ's reputation, not my own; (7) I can be trusted to fulfill a ministry delegated to me; (8) I can be counted upon to correct false doctrine in others; (9) I care enough about others to shed tears for their difficulties; (10) My faith is unfeigned/sincere; (11) I use the gifts God has given to me.

In the discussion, call for your learners to identify relevant text verses for their decisions. You may prefer to give your learners a graded scale for their responses:

- Yes, always/totally.
- Yes, most of the time.
- No, most of the time.
- No, never.

Such a choice may make responding easier.

The God Who Says Yes

Ideally, in every unit of study, the class member's prayer life will reflect the truths being learned from session to session. In a series of character studies, the learner will see images of the kind of person God wants him or her to be or not be. Sincere, persistent petition to God for his help to those ends is always appropriate.

Sometimes this goal is best served from negative examples, such as the foolish rich man of Mark 10 or Pilate. Though adults must see a bit of themselves in those two, no one truly wants to be compared with either one. Suggesting a format of prayer expression for such a lesson could be very helpful. Consider: "God of justice and righteousness, I am sorry that I am like _____. Help me to resist the temptations to be _____. Give me the grace to become _____. Be merciful to me, a sinner." Fill in the first blank with the name of the character. A group reflection on words that fill the other two blanks could well be profitable. For the rich man, words such as *materialistic* and *generous* could fill the blanks respectively. For Pilate, the words *purely pragmatic* and a *person of godly integrity* are possible.

Of course, a similar pattern could be used in lessons on those who have a positive witness. For example, a study of Elizabeth and Zechariah would lend itself to a prayer with the following form: "God who hears and answers prayer, help me to be like _____ in my _____. Help me to avoid the appearance of _____." If done for Zechariah, such words as "in my faithful service," and "the appearance of doubt." For Elizabeth, the words could be "in my submissiveness," and "the appearance of shame at your work in my life" (see Luke 1:24).

The Simple and Profound Choice

James Russell Lowell (1819–1891) expressed it poetically and perfectly in the nineteenth century:

> Once to ev'ry man and nation
> Comes the moment to decide,
> In the strife of truth with falsehood,
> For the good or evil side;
> Some great cause, some great decision,
> Off'ring each the bloom or blight,
> And the choice goes by forever
> 'Twixt that darkness and that light.

Yes or no? That is the question each must ask. That is the decision each must make. The Christian teacher's job is to help all students within his or her sway to make the right one.

YOUR SEVEN DAYS

Taking Advantage of All the Time Available

for Lesson Preparation

by Brent L. Amato

It's Saturday night. You must teach an adult class on Sunday morning, but you've waited until today to begin preparing your lesson. You were going to start earlier, but something came up that took more time than you had planned. Now time is short; and besides that, you're stuck on something. "I had seven days," you say to yourself. "Why did I put off preparing?" Does this sound like you?

An Issue of Stewardship

Teaching, like other activities of life, is an opportunity to glorify God (1 Corinthians 10:31). We are to be good stewards of how we use the gift of teaching, as we are to be good stewards of all our spiritual gifts (1 Peter 4:10). Each of us will give an account to the master teacher for each lesson that we teach (2 Corinthians 5:10). When that time comes, I want to hear those words, "Well done, good and faithful servant! You have been faithful" (Matthew 25:21). I am sobered to know that teachers are held to a higher standard (see James 3:1).

All this makes me ponder what I will do with the time between lessons. When do I start preparing for the next Bible lesson that I am to teach? What does good stewardship say about my seven days?

An Issue of Diligence

As Timothy was urged to be diligent in his ministry (1 Timothy 4:15), we are to exercise diligence in preparing our lessons. Will we make the most of every preparation opportunity (Ephesians 5:15, 16)? Will our preparation time include diligent prayer (1 Thessalonians 5:17)? Will our preparation include intensive study of and meditation on God's Word (Psalm 1:1, 2; 119:15)? Will we prepare so that our learners will end up with a clear understanding of the truths of the lesson (Nehemiah 8:8)? Will we prepare in such a diligent way that we will not speak hastily during the lesson (Proverbs 29:20)? What will we do with our seven days?

An Issue of Quality

We live in a culture of instant gratification and quick fixes. The quicker we get one thing done, the quicker we can move on to something else. Witness the popularity of microwave ovens and fast-food restaurants. This mind-set can leak over into our approach to lesson preparation if we're not careful.

Think about the difference. Would you rather eat a prepackaged frozen dinner that has been zapped quickly in a microwave oven or a dish that has simmered all day in a slow cooker? Aren't frozen dinners and fast food admittedly inferior, popular only because of our crowded schedules? When you gather for Thanksgiving dinner, when you have a special guest for dinner, when everything has to be "just right," what kind of meal do you serve? How much time goes into its preparation? Don't your learners deserve that same kind of attention as you prepare the spiritual food that you will serve on Sunday morning?

An Issue of Percolation

Starting your preparation on Sunday afternoon for the following Sunday morning's lesson results in a process I call "percolating the lesson." Starting preparation on Sunday afternoon will result in an awareness of things going on around you. Over seven days you will be watching and listening for God to drop insights, large and small. Lessons are refined and improved over time. New ideas occur; material is focused, changed, even discarded; creativity blossoms!

So Sunday afternoon is not too early to begin! You may spend only a few minutes on Sunday, just long enough to read the lesson text along with its background text and to jot down a couple of ideas that come to mind. Then take time to pray about the upcoming lesson. That is something you'll want to do each day. *If you do nothing more than pray every day about your lesson, you will improve your teaching!*

On Monday through Saturday, take a few minutes each day to add to the lesson. Research the historical background. Explore a commentary or two. Some commentaries are great with the exegesis; others are excellent devotional commentaries. Use both kinds if you can. Think about the kinds of resources you will need; plan ahead to have them available. Notice what's leading the news every night; how does your lesson text speak to the issues of the day? And pray each day about the lesson, about the students who will be participating, and about your own spiritual growth. If you find just 30-45 minutes each day, Monday through Saturday, you will have added three to more than four hours to your initial time spent on Sunday preparing for your lesson. And you didn't have to cram that into 10–2 Saturday night!

Using Ready-made Curriculum

"But I use a curriculum that does all that stuff for me!" you may protest. I don't have to do all that research and study; my lesson commentary has it all there for me already. That's a good start, but every lesson needs to become your own lesson. Here are some easy ideas for how to do that.

Begin on Sunday the same as above. During the week, be sure to read the Scriptures suggested in your lesson commentary for daily Bible reading. If you are following the Uniform Series, these readings have been carefully selected to prepare you for the upcoming lesson. Expand on what your lesson commentary has with independent research. Adapt the discussion questions and the learning activities to suit your own students and their particular situation. Pay attention to the news and connect the lesson with what's happening in real time. (Most dated curriculum is produced months—if not years—ahead of the dates the lessons are used. Making the lessons timely is on you!) And pray every day for God to use your preparation and presentation to make the impact he desires in the lives of your students.

We all know that a Saturday night or a Sunday morning sometimes "blows up" in a teacher's face because of the unexpected stuff of life. A Saturday night emergency can easily rob you of time to prepare your lesson! Starting to prepare sooner rather than later is a wonderful hedge against such challenges.

When I come home from church each Sunday, I have three options: (1) take a nap (2) watch sports on TV, or (3) spend a few minutes on next week's lesson. Seven days. How will I spend them?

Your Spiritual Life
Growing and Modeling

by James Riley Estep, Jr.

The teacher of geometry needs to know geometry and teaching methods. If he knows those two things, it matters not how he lives his life; he can still effectively communicate the axioms and theorems and produce students who know geometry.

The teacher of the Bible needs to know the Bible and teaching methods. But she must have more as well. She must live by the principles she would teach to others. Teaching Sunday school is not merely an exercise in communicating facts; it is a shared adventure in following Christ. And as someone has said, "You cannot lead where you have not already walked." This means that teachers must be constantly in tune with the condition of their spiritual lives.

Overview of Three Domains

Spiritual maturity (or lack of it) manifests itself in three ways: Christian worldview (life of the mind), Christian experience (heart), and Christian service (hands). We may refer to these as the *cognitive, affective,* and *active* domains of spiritual maturity, respectively.

We see these three reflected in Scripture. It is said of one of the Old Testament's most recognized teachers, "Ezra had devoted himself to the study and observance of the Law of the Lord, and to teaching its decrees and laws" (Ezra 7:10). Notice that Ezra didn't teach until he had prepared his heart (affective), had sought the law (cognitive), and had put his faith into practice (active).

This model has found many contemporary expressions in Christian literature and within congregations. We grow in spiritual maturity through study (sharpening our Christian intellect, our life of the mind), devotion (heart), and service (putting faith into active practice).

The Domain of the Mind

Bible teachers have to study in preparing their lessons. This study, of course, aids the teacher's own spiritual development. However, it is a mistake to assume that lesson preparation is sufficient to promote your own spiritual maturity in the domain of the mind. Teachers should make sure they are *being* taught. Self-study of Scripture is a good thing, but you should also be part of a group where you are the student, learning from another. Furthermore, your personal study of Scripture should not be limited to lesson preparation, but should include study for personal benefit.

The Domain of the Heart

Teachers should also have a regular practice of devotion. "Having daily devotions" does not simply refer to personal Bible study. Rather, it means practicing spiritual disciplines such as prayer, fasting, personal worship, and journaling. Some teachers neglect this dimension of their spiritual lives, substituting lesson preparation time for personal devotion. This is a mistake.

Having an established practice of devotion, perhaps by using a devotional or prayer guide, helps the teacher center his or her inner life (heart) on God. This happens not only in a daily "quiet time" of devotions, but also in a group setting. The sharing that happens in the context of relationships can benefit the spiritual lives of everyone present.

The Domain of Service

Yes, teaching is your service, and being a teacher aids in the promotion of your spiritual life. But how about also committing yourself to acts of service outside of your teaching role? Many adult Bible study classes not only gather to learn, but also schedule opportunities for their class members to serve in the church and community on a regular basis.

Dual Concern

Teachers should have a dual concern for their spiritual lives. Primarily, we are to be concerned for our own growing and deepening relationship with God through Jesus Christ. However, we must also be concerned with how our spiritual maturity is modeled to others. The teacher should serve as an example of one who is maturing in Christ in all three domains. That too is part of teaching.

SCRIPTURE INDEX

SCRIPTURE INDEX

Scripture Index

TOPICAL INDEX

TOPICAL INDEX